COMPASSIONATE COMMUNICATING BECAUSE
MOMENTS MATTER:

POETRY, PROSE, AND PRACTICES

Kimberly Pearce

COMPASSIONATE COMMUNICATING BECAUSE MOMENTS MATTER:
POETRY, PROSE, AND PRACTICE

This book is published by Lulu Enterprises, Inc. To purchase copies or for information, visit www.lulu.com.

The photograph on the book cover was taken by Kimberly Pearce in Phuket, Thailand in 2009.

FIRST PRINTING

November, 2012

ISBN: 978-1-300-31833-0

This book is an "unexpected pregnancy." Three years ago, my husband Barnett Pearce and I were planning to write a book about spiritual practices for making more compassionate and loving social worlds. We did two workshops on the topic, we had a clear and elaborate outline for the book, and we felt we had some useful things to say. He died before we broke the page and I knew that the book we dreamed about would not be written.

Six months after his death, I awoke one morning and said, "it's time to write." The clarity of the thought surprised me especially since I had no plans for writing the book that you are about to read. Without an outline, or an audience in mind, or an idea of what I would be writing except to know that it was about mindfulness and compassion of our social worlds, I started to write. I think of this book as a delightfully surprising unexpected pregnancy and birth that I have welcomed with open arms. I hope you will too.

This book combines my very real and personal life journey with tested models and concepts that can help us make more mindful selves, more compassionate and loving relationships, and better social worlds. Some of the ideas in this book are at the edge of my own learning and development, so you will find me stammering and using poetry and metaphor to point to what I can't yet say clearly. The pregnancy and birth continue and I hope that those of you who read this will add to what I'm not yet able to clearly articulate.

As I worked on this book I had many wonderful conversation partners whose voices have strengthened my own. My S.P. Gang, your lives inspire me and what we are making together is at the heart of this book. Thank you!! My dear and long-time friend Catherine Swanson has been an inspiring conversation partner as we have scaled the mountains and valleys of our lives together, using, among other things, the lens of communication theory, interpersonal neurobiology, and adult developmental learning to deepen our thinking and to grow our hearts. Thank you Casey for reading and commenting on the last draft of this book. Special thanks to Marit Eikaas Haavimb, Don Marrs, Linda Blong, John Stewart, and Tim Thomas for reading various versions of the book and for providing such thoughtful and useful suggestions. John, your comment to me after reading the first chapter, "Beam me up Scottie" makes me laugh to this day. I especially appreciate your keen mind and your full-throated responses to these ideas. I'm especially indebted to Jesse Sostrin, Philipe Thomas, Erin Kreeger, and Jan Elliott. The four of you have spent many hours providing detailed and specific comments that have given me perspective and clarity when I needed it. You will find your voices in this book as well. Thank you for walking this journey with me. Holly Peterson and I began working together on formatting and artistic designs when I published my most recent book of poetry. She has the skills and ability to take words on a page and imbue them with artistry and grace. I asked her to do the same in this book. Thank you Holly for your creative touches!

The only person who has been by my side all 54 years of my life is my mom, Linda Whittington. Not only is she my "precious Mama" but she is also my best friend. We have been through many lives together and I suspect that we will experience many more before it's all said and done. She read the first draft of this book and, as a result, we revisited some early and painful life experiences together. But we did it with deep love and compassion and we are both better people because of that. Thank you Mama for loving me as you have. This book is dedicated to you.

Kim Pearce

October 11, 2012

Oracle, Arizona

CONTENTS

SECTION 1: DREAMS, POETRY, AND COMMUNICATION THEORY

SECTION 2: PRACTICES

1

SECTION 1: DREAMS, POETRY, AND COMMUNICATION THEORY

The first sentence of every novel should be: Trust me, this will take time but there is order here, very faint, very human. Meander if you want to get to town.

–Michael Ondaatje

Introduction

Why This Book?

This book is not a novel. But what you are about to read reminds me of the quote by Ondaatje. There is order to the ideas in this book but they are very faint and very human. And to the extent that you meander, you will see more on your way to town.

This is a book about mindfulness and awareness. It's about awareness of our social worlds and the part that each of us plays in making those worlds, one conversation at a time. It's also a book about compassion and its importance in making healthier selves, relationships, and social worlds. And similar to anything that one sets out to master, mindfulness and the enactment of compassion require practice. And lots of it...every day! So this is also a book of practices to enhance your mindfulness of our social worlds and your part in helping to make fuller expressions of compassion in your daily life and with people not like you.

Our walk into town begins at home. I'm sitting in my courtyard, a warm breeze is running its fingers through my palm plant making its long strands of hair dance in the wind, while the pure sound of my wind chimes strikes deep, resonant, and beautiful chords. My dog Luke is lying next to me, his chest rising and falling to the steady movement of his slow, deep breaths.

All of this is occurring in the same moment as less desirable, frightening, and destructive happenings—a bloody civil war in Syria, a bloody political battle here in the United States, people like you and me desperate for work, or a safe place to live, or a loving relationship of which to be a part. I am holding the range of these realities as well as my own severed heart that feels the ache of the physical death only seven months ago of my husband and soul mate, Barnett.

There is a part of the "physical me" that can feel the differences in my body when I'm reflecting on the sights and sounds of sitting in my beautiful and peaceful courtyard (an open and relaxed body), when I imagine the horrors of war and being a civilian in the middle of it (bodily tightness and fear responses), when I think of people who are over matched by their current circumstances of unemployment, financial instability, feeling alone and without resources, or whatever the circumstances may be (tightness and heaviness in the chest, shallow breathing) and the physical death of my husband (unregulated bodily functions). Our bodies are finely tuned instruments that remind us how we're doing in something other than words.

For most of us, how we're doing depends on what's in front of us or what we are attending to. If we are paying close attention, we find our moods shift sometimes dramatically and within minutes. We feel centered and grounded in this moment but that person whom we dislike has just walked in the room and the ground has now shifted to quick sand, or we have said or done something that we regret, and the unrelenting and loathing self-talk just won't leave us alone. Experiencing the push and pull of simultaneous yet contradictory emotions and ways of acting into the next moment are the daily stuff of our lives. Welcome to the human condition!

And yet there are some among us who have spent their lives practicing a different way of experiencing and living into the human condition. There are many names for it, but as a placeholder, I'm calling it "*living* compassion and love" or "*being* compassion and love." Jesus instructed His followers to love their enemies, to turn the other cheek, and to do good to those who seek to do them harm. These were not just idle words; Jesus consistently showed compassion to the poor, disenfranchised, and outcasts and His way of being in the world pointed to nothing less than a new social order characterized by social justice, compassion and love. More recently, the Dalai Lama met with a Buddhist monk who had been imprisoned in China for 30 years. When asked if he had ever feared for his life the monk said, "yes, twice. Both times I was afraid that I was losing my ability to experience compassion for the guards who were torturing me." Wow! This is a qualitatively different aspect and experience of the human condition.

It can be easy to interpret these expressions of compassion and love as drawing a clear boundary that does not make room for less flattering emotional experiences like anger, contempt, disgust, and rage.   Please do not hear me as suggesting this. Experiencing our humanness involves the integration of a full, and wildly contrasting, range of emotions and experiences. The question for me is how compassion and love intertwine and work together with emotions we might label as "the shadow"? As my friend Erin has reminded me, Buddhist teacher Pema Chodron talks about unconditional openness in this way:

> "The peace that we're looking for is not peace that crumbles
> as soon as there is difficulty or chaos. Whether we're
> seeking inner peace or global peace or a combination of the
> two, the way to experience it is to build on the foundation
> of unconditional openness to all that arises. Peace isn't an
> experience free of challenges, free of rough and smooth, it's
> an experience that's expansive enough to include all that
> arises without feeling threatened."[1]

I want to substitute compassion for peace and repeat that compassion "isn't an experience free of challenges, free of rough and smooth, it's an experience that's expansive enough *to include all that arises without feeling threatened.*

Why should we spend time attempting to cultivate this level of compassion? My response to questions like this is we are living in a historical epoch in which the humanness expressed in people like Jesus and the Buddhist monk imprisoned for 30 years is the next evolutionary jump that more of us need to live into. Compassion is not just an "internal emotional experience." Rather it is a way of being with others that makes a space for something new to emerge. The "something new" that compassion makes possible is essential at this moment in history for two primary reasons. The first is that our world is now materially, socially, economically, and technologically so inextricably interdependent that what we do matters. Ninety seven percent of climatologists believe global climate change is occurring at a much faster pace than would normally occur because of green house gases being emitted at alarming rates in countries like the United States and China. World economic markets rise and fall because of the economic health and policies of large and small countries around the world. Oil production in one region of the world affects gas prices half a world away. And small-scale conflicts can quickly turn into regional conflicts that can quickly become large-scale conflicts. As I write this, an amateur anti-Islamic video has gone viral on the internet and 20 countries around the world are in their third day of violent protests. The capacity for the escalation of these kinds of conflicts leads me to the second reason for more of us needing to enact lives of compassion: humans now have the capacity to destroy life as we know it on this planet. As I write this, eight countries have previously detonated nuclear weapons and Iran is moving closer to having this capability. Israel is publicly chastising the United States administration for not drawing a clear line in the sand for a preemptive strike on Iran. And no doubt this public debate will expand to other nations.

These two realities make "the way we express our humanness" very important. Critics will say that these global-scale issues have little or nothing to do with how you and I communicate. These are issues of power and privilege and policy and inequality. My response is yes and...every one of these global issues is also about relationships and the patterns of communication that occur leading us to adopt decision x rather than decision y. There was a time in history when the societal norm was to treat women as chattel and blacks as less than human. And now most of us shudder at the thought of how these groups were abused. Large-scale shifts in societal thinking and evolving laws that reflect them begin with changes in the hearts and minds of people like you and me.

I also believe that we have the capacity to grow our hearts and minds so as to live and enact compassion every day. It is not out of any one's reach and it is not primarily for the saints among us. These daily acts aren't just "feel good emotions" for the practitioner (although there is empirical evidence that links the increase of "feel good" chemicals serotonin and dopamine into our nervous system during compassionate and loving states), but they create the fertile soil for better relationships. And if enough of us are living lives of compassion, our families, our organizations, our communities, and, yes, even our societies will be stronger. But I have no illusions that this is an easy shift to make. In fact, it is a life-long commitment to a daily set of practices (and thankfully there are practices from a plethora of traditions from which to choose). This book is for those of you who, like me, are curious enough to explore, commit and hopefully live into this kind of humanness.

This book is divided into the two sections. The first section consisting of chapters 1-4, sets out ideas through dreams, images, poetry...and communication theory (yes, one of these things is not like the others!). I'm trying to say things in this section about compassion and communication that are difficult to put into words so you will find me moving in and out of prose and poetry. But don't be put off by the use of communication theory. I think you will find that this lens to view and understand communication will enrich what I am pointing to in poetry and metaphor. I hope that the various ways of attempting to say what, in many respects, is unsayable will be useful rather than distracting. Keep in mind that in these chapters we'll be "meandering" as we get to town. Section 2, chapters 5-9, builds on the ideas of the first section but shifts the focus from words and images to practice. Each chapter provides specific practices to increase our ability (individually and collectively) to experience and express compassion.

Taken together, I hope this book provides useful new ways of thinking and acting into your social worlds.

A Dream

Have you ever had an ah-ha moment or experience that changed you from the "inside-out"? You knew at the time that this experience was significant and every moment thereafter will bear witness to its significance? I have had a few of these experiences. The one that I want to share with you was an all-night lucid dream that occurred on February 18, 2011. At the time I was 52.

By way of context, I had been feeling quite inarticulate off and on for quite some time. This has been a recurring theme for me over many years; the ocean waves that come in cycles is an apt metaphor for my experience and the story I've told myself of my inability to speak well. Some days are better than others and, like the ocean swells, the experience inside my skin is that my ability to speak well varies depending on the currents in my life. The night before my dream the Board of the CMM Institute that my husband Barnett and I co-founded, had a conference call meeting and I was having a very difficult time expressing myself coherently or well.

I shared these feelings with Barnett over dinner, not for the purpose of solving a problem but of naming and exploring the experiences with a trusted partner and friend. He asked if I was able to celebrate my strengths. "Yes, I said. I'm not feeling bad about myself as much as feeling vulnerable." Thankfully, at this stage of my life I can hold the complexity of my many selves (strengths and weaknesses) without too much contempt or judgment. This particular area elicited a profound feeling of vulnerability more than judgment. But those feelings of vulnerability disturbed me.

A few hours later we went to bed and I had a full night of this lucid dream. The dream had two parts: during the first half of the night I relived three important stages in my life and I was completely embodying and experiencing myself during each stage. The stages that I relived included experiences I had as a child, as a young woman in my twenties, and as a more mature 50 year old. The second part of the dream was "instruction" about the significance of the dream for understanding issues that include all of humanity.

The three stages of my life that I relived in the dream make sense only if you know the larger contexts in which these snapshots occurred. Consequently, I'll be providing background information about the people, places, and time frame of these stages followed by what I experienced as I was dreaming.

THE DREAM: PART 1

The dream began when I was between the ages of 8 to 10.

Background: I had a very frightening and constant set of experiences during these 2 years. My mom had married Steve, a man whom she met at the grocery store where she worked. Steve had experienced his own hell as a child and, I believe, he had never fully recovered. When he was 15 years old, his father murdered his mother and committed suicide. Steve found them both in their bedroom. As the oldest of 5 children, he attempted to keep the siblings together, so they were sent to an orphanage rather than foster homes. When something that traumatic happens, a person and a family must make sense of the experience and somehow integrate it into their current life. Steve's response was to drink; and he was a hard-core alcoholic. Our family dynamic during these years included dramatic yelling and fighting. The three of us fought almost every day…and the fights could be ugly. I remember one night being served liver for dinner. I didn't want to eat it but I was told that I could not leave the table until I had eaten everything on my plate. I sat motionless at the table staring at my plate. At one point, Steve swept his arm across the table, sending everything crashing to the floor. I was terrified of his anger.

My biological father was also an alcoholic and I was court-mandated to spend every other weekend with him. He lived in a triplex with his parents. Like my father, my grandfather was also a heavy drinker and, without exception, the weekends that I stayed with my dad included the nightly ritual of my dad and grandfather getting drunk, getting belligerent, and screaming at each other. I remember pleading with my mom to not make me go to my dad's because I was so afraid of their anger. But my home with my mom and Steve was also a very frightening place.

I don't remember what the precipitating event was but, at 10 years of age, I packed my bags and announced to my mom that I was running away from home. I walked about a mile to my maternal grandparents house; my mom left our apartment later that afternoon and joined me at my grandparents where we stayed for a few days. A few weeks later my mom began the divorce proceedings and Steve moved out of our apartment. I learned years later that Steve had threatened to kill my mom and me if she left him. It was one reason she stayed in this relationship for two years. Given his own experience of seeing the horror of his dead parents in their bedroom, it wasn't unthinkable that Steve could have done the same to my mom and me.

The Dream: I relived these experiences in my dream and felt the terror and utter vulnerability of that little girl. As I saw myself experiencing these very scary feelings, I realized that I didn't have the maturity or the ability to language these feelings and experiences. I didn't have a voice to express the terror of these experiences. But I did have a body that felt the frightfulness of my environment and I acted out these fears in the way I knew how, by arguing and misbehaving and eventually running away. In this part of the dream, I lived my muteness and the utter terror of being at the mercy of angry and out of control adults in my life. For the first time Kim the dreamer could recognize that I didn't have a voice. Consequently, I saw how these very scary experiences *lived in me* because I didn't have the language to get outside of them.

The dream then jumped to the decade of my twenties.

Background: Among other things, this was a time in my life in which I could articulate how inarticulate I felt. I met, dated, and eventually married a man who was 7 years my senior. He was smart, charming, very witty, and articulate. I was 19 when we met and we dated for six stormy years that could be characterized as an on-again, off-again relationship. After a particularly painful breakup in which I told him that I never wanted to see him again, we cautiously began corresponding several months later and eventually married; I was 26 when we married.

One of the themes of our life together was his relentless criticism of me. He would criticize my dress, my speech, my lack of wit and inability to banter. And for most of the decade of my twenties I believed him; I thought his criticisms were warranted and if only I could be more articulate and witty and bright, he would love me unconditionally. The interesting thing was we would talk about this and during those conversations I was very clear and articulate with penetrating analyses of the situation. But in daily life I lacked the clarity and ease that he so wished that I would possess. I remember how destructive these criticisms were; there was a point in my life when I had a difficult time stringing words together into a coherent sentence, I was so tied up in knots. This was a decade in which *his stories about me* were the stories that I lived. I internalized his criticisms and saw them as "the truth."

There was a clarifying moment when I was 30 (and I mean clarifying "moment"). The insight occurred as if the heavens had parted and a diagram of our relationship had dropped from the sky. I saw the "pattern" in our relationship and the ways in which his pathologies and mine meshed together to form a pattern that was figuratively and literally killing me/us. We sat down and I told him about the pattern that was now so clear to me of his putting me in unwinnable situations to test my devotion, and my wanting to show him that I could change and become the person that he wanted me to be, and our family histories that drove and elicited these behaviors. That moment of clarity unshackled the albatross around my neck. In that instant, I had "a voice" that I hadn't lived into before and I moved from being the "subject" of my husband's story of me to the "author" of my story of me. It also was the beginning of the end of our marriage.

The Dream: In my dream, I was embodying the pain of that young woman as she was living and storying her inability to be the articulate and quick-witted person that her husband so wished she could be. It was similar to the vulnerability she experienced as the young girl, although now she was mature enough to articulate her inarticulateness and the pain and insecurity that this caused. Although she could speak about this and thus get some emotional distance from it, she was still trapped in her desire to be smarter, wittier, and more pleasing to her husband. She was trying so hard to be loved and to be the person her husband wanted her to be. Instead there was a knot in the pit of her stomach and a heart that was broken.

Background: From my thirties to age 50, my voice was strong, clear, and, even sometimes, articulate. But when it wasn't, I didn't feel bad about myself like I had in my twenties. I attribute this to the "ah-ha" moment when I was 30, to the subsequent work I did to name and understand the ways that my earlier experiences had shaped me, and to a mature, life-giving, and loving relationship that my second husband Barnett and I were making. We were best friends, lovers, colleagues, partners... and very supportive of the complexity of the selves that we had become. We genuinely liked, respected, and loved each other. We didn't try to change each other EVER; instead we constantly celebrated one another and our relationship, foibles and all. When I was 50 Barnett was diagnosed with terminal cancer. In a single moment it was as if the safe and secure place that was our lives was shattered.

The Dream: My dream jumped from the young woman in her twenties to the 50 year-old who heard her husband's death sentence for the first time. My body was unable to regulate itself. I had continual hot flashes and waves of uncontrollable crying. I was reliving these intense emotions in my dream and in this lucid dream state I was living the uncontrollable grief that expressed itself in tears: I was sobbing. I felt an existential vulnerability much like the vulnerability I experienced as a little girl. At 50 in this unthinkable situation, I lost my voice again... and as the 52 year-old woman who just hours before was telling her husband about her feelings of inarticulateness, I saw that I was living again into the vulnerability of a situation in which I had no voice.

In my lucid dream state, existential vulnerability was a recurring pattern for this little girl become woman. And just as I was able to see and name that, the dream shifted abruptly; I was no longer the "embodied Kim" of these time periods, but rather a Benevolent Witness to her life. As I watched Kim from a more expansive perspective, I saw the same experiences and life story that I had just experienced in the dream. But this time, and from a different vantage point, I felt overwhelming love and compassion for her. And that love and compassion was not just for her, it was for all of the people in the dream...and beyond. This love and compassion was for all life forms...and it filled the universe. The details of Kim's lived and told story are hers but the themes throughout the dream of vulnerability, of muteness, of family patterns that are often (usually) out of awareness but, nonetheless, cast very long shadows, of wanting and needing safety and love...these are themes about our human condition.

I believe that this Witness provided a window into a reality that is always there but that few of us come to *really know*. I was seeing (my) life through a lens and experience of Mystery and awe and wonder. I'm using words like Witness and Mystery here as a placeholder for an experience that can variously and inadequately be named as divine love, oneness, union, etc. Seeing through this lens was a qualitative shift of mind. And this way of seeing made all the difference!

In the poem that you are about to read, notice the allusion to two qualities of mind—one that captures our attention while keeping us shackled and the other that knows something much more profound about the human condition. Interestingly, Rumi is suggesting that love, or what I have called Mystery, is the "game changer."

The Nothing of Roselight

Death comes, and what we thought

we needed loses importance.

The living shiver, focused

on a muscular dark hand,

rather than the glowing cup it holds,

or the toast being proposed.

In that same way love enters

your life, and the I, the ego,

a corrupt, self-absorbed king,

dies during the night.

Let him go.

Breathe cold new air,

the nothing of roselight.

--*Rumi*

The Witness in my dream that sees and holds the totality of Kim's life and *all life forms at every stage with an all encompassing love and compassion* could also be named the death of the ego. When that death comes, what we thought we needed loses importance!

THE DREAM: PART 2, INSTRUCTION

When I, as seen through the lens of Benevolent Witness, saw life unfolding in love and compassion my dream shifted dramatically again, but this time the shift was from Witness to analysis and instruction.

Obviously dreams can be understood and interpreted on many levels. A recurring theme during the second half of the night was the "dissolution of self," or the death of the ego, as Rumi calls it in the poem that you just read. Personal development, or more complex ways of knowing and being in the world, create "ruptures" in how we experience and hold our identity. In one respect, personal development creates the scaffolding for more sophisticated and complex ways of naming, holding, and experiencing "me." So for example, one way of measuring personal and social development is that the capacity for holding complexity, difference, and diversity—or what is not me—increases. And this is a good thing because to the extent that I can see and hold the complexity of me, I can do the same for you and vise versa. Having said that, until we are able to experience our self and others as the Benevolent Witness in my dream was able to—as "no self" or "self that is one with the universe"—we will continue to know and live in existential vulnerability. This may seem obvious, but the "ah ha" learning for me is that as we are on the road to maturing (and in some cases, becoming quite mature!) into more complex ways of living into a reality of unity, profound vulnerability will continue to be part of our "individual and social apparel."

The instruction continued... And because this is the case, it is imperative that, as we are able, we hold our self and each other in a space of compassion and love.

Commentary about this instruction: I'm struck by the circularity of this. There is a reality of oneness that is infused with Love. Until you and I know this like we know other taken-for-granted aspects of our existence (like the sun will rise in the East) we will experience the rupture of this unity causing, among other things, existential vulnerability. This rupture in unity will be more apparent and painful depending on where we are in the process of our evolution. But where ever you and I are in this process, practice as much love and compassion as we are able. In other words, to the extent that we live "as if" we already know the reality that already exists, we will more fully manifest a reality that already exists... even if we don't quite know it yet.

Phew. This makes my head hurt. It also makes me think of a line in T.S. Eliot's *Four Quartets* that has stayed with me, even though I read it for the first time 30 years ago:

We shall not cease from exploration

And the end of all our exploring

Will be to arrive where we started

And know the place for the first time.

Perhaps this work that we're doing to enact love and compassion is helping us move toward the arrival of where we started and knowing the place for the first time. The beginning was oneness—the universe and everything in it came from the same source, starting with the Mystery of the big bang: one moment there was nothing... and then there was everything that has made the evolution of the universe and life as we know it possible. If we truly understand this and take it in, we will see that interconnectedness and oneness at all levels is the reality of our existence.

Because the reality of oneness is not the reality that most of us experience in our daily lives, remembering to use the lens of

Mystery that I described earlier is crucial in helping us to hold the fragility and vulnerability of "ourselves as becoming" with humility, love and compassion. The Mystery, or said differently, Love filling the universe, that I experienced in my dream when I stepped outside of myself to view the totality of my life, was a Big M Mystery consciousness of a "not me" embracing, loving, holding close the "vulnerable me" and the "vulnerable human condition." The not me and the vulnerable me/human condition were one.

The morning after this dream, a poem wrote itself:

Baby's Breath

> We are time travelers
>
> you and I,
>
> clothed in this body
>
> of flesh and blood
>
> but able to sing
>
> the praises of star-studded galaxies.
>
>
> Mystery parades through
>
> unfathomable light years
>
> But watch closely...
>
> it kisses us on the cheek.
>
>
> This consciousness ignites a longing
>
> that will not die,
>
> but its unfolding is not easy.
>
>
> Birth only comes in the
>
> excruciating pains of labor.
>
> But when the new form arrives

the pain quickly

becomes a distant memory.

While the pain is most intense

look for the gift.

When you untie the bow and open the box

Love and compassion await.

This poem takes me back to Pema Chodron's statement to "build on the foundation of unconditional openness to all that arises." ...While the pain is most intense, look for the gift...

Before moving on, reflect with me for a moment on these phrases: Consciousness ignites a longing...but its unfolding is not easy....While the pain is most intense, look for the gift...love and compassion await. All themes of the "embodied, vulnerable Kim throughout her life" and the instruction during the second part of the Dream, that love and compassion enfold us...*always*.

2

Reflections on the Dream Through Images

So what did this lucid dream teach me and how has it changed my life? Let me respond by first saying that what I'm about to write needs to be heard in "stammers and stutters." What I experienced is not easily put into a string of words that form thoughts and sentences (I guess I'm back to being inarticulate, but this time with the playful recognition that ineffability is the first, and perhaps ultimately the only, response to Mystery.) Remember we are meandering on our way to town.

With that caveat, here is my summary of learnings from my very powerful dream:

The reality of the Universe and everything in it is oneness;

Our task (individually and collectively) is to know deep in our bones and in our every breath that, whatever else we might say about our individual and collective evolution, compassion and love infuse it;

Viewed through the lens of Mystery or the Benevolent Witness, human brokenness, suffering, and wholeness are equally, compassionately, and lovingly held;

We are not loved more deeply as we evolve and become more loving...but our capacity to experience Love expands as we mature. Our work of evolution is NOT about becoming more lovable, but of knowing that, in the context of Mystery, every stage of development is held in a compassionate and loving embrace;

Our evolution is "personal" and "social." This means that our evolutionary task is to lovingly embrace and compassionately hold all of the MEs, from birth until death, and to lovingly embrace and to compassionately hold all of the OTHERS whom you have, will, or may never encounter, from birth until death. To the extent that we can do this, we are supporting human evolution and living into the oneness of reality that already exists;

Regardless of where you are in your personal evolutionary journey, it's OK. This is not about winning a contest —it's about *participating* in an evolutionary *process* that is currently giving birth to the enactment of love and compassion on a global scale.

I have just read over these points and it seems more ethereal than I mean it to sound. So let me acknowledge that and say a bit more about my learnings.

The experience of this dream gave me a more expansive framework for the non-dreaming aspects of my life. Another way of saying this is my frame of reference across contexts and situations is much larger and, by extension, more loving and compassionate. My heart is more open. I have especially noticed this enlarged frame in the way I have experienced Barnett's illness and death. Let me illustrate in poetry; this poem came to me in an especially difficult time of grieving shortly after Barnett's passing:

Visitation

I was having

a difficult day

taking care of the

defective water pump, the

broken electrical switch in the garage,

and my unhappy phone that was well past

retirement.

All reminders that my partner

is not here.

...And then He came to me

and said that

I am not alone...

that We are not alone.

The veil that separates

one form from another

is sheerer

than we think.

If we stay open to Mystery

what feels like an amputation

becomes just a change of venue

Barnett did come to me and I think I was able to receive him and what he had to say because I was open to Mystery. As a result of the dream, I'm holding the grieving Kim much more compassionately. As a result I think she is able to *receive* the compassionate and loving embrace of others (others currently living as well as those who have passed on) in a more profound way. I'm also finding that compassionately holding my broken heart and spirit is opening my heart more fully to the broken heart and spirit in others. And all of us live, in one form or another, with broken hearts.

This leads to a final take-away that I'd like to describe: it has something to do with our stance towards others. The metaphor that comes to me is moving from a tightened fist (something about wanting to control or protect myself) to an outstretched, or at least an open, hand. We in the West live in an individualistic culture. It gets expressed and reinforced in many ways—here is one that I chanted as a kid when I was teased: "sticks and stones may break my bones but names will never hurt me". But, of course, the reality is that the way we are with each other matters. And every one of us has or is currently wrestling with compassionately loving ourselves because of what others have said or how we've been treated. Words do hurt, unhealthy patterns get made in one context and repeat themselves in other contexts, and scar tissue develops...in the heart...in the mind... and throughout the body and spirit. I was recently thinking about this and about how healing it is to be in the presence of someone who shows compassion and love. The definition of "heal" is to form healthy flesh again, and to unite after being cut or broken. We need to remember how much of our lives occur through "mimicked contact"; of observing how others "do life" and finding ourselves mimicking what we see.

Tracks in the Road

> The warmer than usual
>
> Winter
>
> has left the Arizona desert
>
> parched
>
> and begging for water.

> And then it came...
>
> First as snow
>
> and then rain,
>
> each drop and flake
>
> falling to earth,
>
> losing its individuality
>
> to become One
>
> with the soil.

> We know that the intercourse
>
> of water and earth
>
> sustains life
>
> and gives birth to new forms.

But the moist soil

is also a

Master Mimic.

Today's lesson-

    Tracks in the road.

A truck has driven

down a dirt road,

the marriage of soil and tread

Creating a

perfect

reproduction

of the over-sized tire.

The now fossilized treads

have left reminders

that the pattern remains

long after the rendezvous has occurred.

We, too, are the

rain, the soil, and

the tracks in the road.

At the moment of contact

let us remember to

Show care

and compassion.

There is something in this learning about a stance of humility about the effects we have on each other. This points to the importance of a quality of mind that is attentive to the unfolding "moments of contact." My friend Jan says that in her Zen practice this is referred to as "experiencing the whole moment whole bodily. I love that image of "whole moment" and "whole bodily."

Sometimes, my walks in nature are instructive about what gets elicited when I'm "whole moment and whole bodily":

Presence

On my walk in the desert today

Nature and I had a love affair.

The cool breeze caressed my face and ran its fingers

through my tousled hair.

The dirt road crackled and sang under the weight of my feet

and the purple and blue wildflowers

slipped through the cracks in the road and

raised their hands in praise.

A lone bird cooed in the background

as the sun did shadow dances with the trees, the distant mountains,

and with me.

These sights, sounds, and caresses make me giddy...

and they make my heart skip a beat.

It is an effortless love affair

I just need to show up and be present.

It makes me wonder…

what daily love affairs

humans would have

if we were

    present like this

      for each other.

OK…if your response to what I've been saying is to scold yourself for not being present enough, or loving enough, or compassionate enough towards yourself or others, or whole moment and whole body enough, you are focused on the more narrow reality of the journey. Enlarge the frame! As Rumi reminds us, "The living shiver, focused on a muscular dark hand, rather than the glowing cup it holds, or the toast being proposed." Focus on the glowing cup and the toast, and the *practice* of imagining looking through the lens of Mystery and you will see that love and compassion have been here all along!

3

An Introduction to CMM

In the previous two chapters, I've tried to say things that are difficult to say; consequently I've used dreams, reflections, and poetry to point to a way of thinking/knowing/being that prose alone can't capture.   But I'm feeling the need to shift to prose.

I realize that many of you might be asking, "what the heck is she trying to say?!" Here's the brief summary; the "cliff notes" if you will: I believe that if we are to meet the challenges we face on our current home, planet Earth, the key evolutionary task for us humans - in this precise moment of history - is to enact love and compassion as our "default" way of being together. These are not just "feel good" emotions although we now know through brain imaging that dopamine and serotonin get released into our bodies. They are *ways of being* that provide the fertile soil for growth, individually and socially. Think about it—in the moments when someone acts compassionately and lovingly towards you, chances are your "self" and your "mind" become more expansive.   Now add that moment to thousands of others…and now let's add more than 6 billion people on the planet. What differences would it make to the sufferings on our planet if these "moments" were closer to the norm? Given the complexity and challenges the world faces, we need bigger, more expansive minds.

I'd like to add Barnett's voice.   As he and I were beginning to work on a book about CMM as Spiritual Practice (we believe the enactment of compassion and love is at the heart of spiritual practice), he said this to me: "it's all about mystery; particularly making mystery the lens through which we view the world. To be spiritually evolved is to live "normally" in an experience of awe, wonder, ineffability, the appreciation of the bigness of it all, and the perception of the oneness of it all."   I would add that to be spiritually evolved is to live, as best as we are able, "normally" in the experience and enactment of compassion and love (think of Jesus and the Buddhist monk that I referred to earlier).

So this is our task. And, as I said earlier, part of the task is to compassionately and lovingly hold your self wherever you are in this evolutionary journey...and to compassionately and lovingly hold others wherever they are in their evolutionary journey. You can't do this on your own; we need the support of each other. And if we're really serious about our personal and social evolution, we need to commit to daily practices that grow our heart and expand our minds. Practice...and support from others!

CMM'S VIEW OF COMMUNICATION

Using and practicing CMM with others is *one way* of expanding our hearts and minds. For those of you who are not familiar with CMM, it is most known as a theory of communication. It is formally called the Coordinated Management of Meaning (CMM) and it was developed in the 1970s by Barnett Pearce and Vern Cronen. CMM has continued to evolve through a cadre of students, researcher and practitioners from around the world. Because of its uses in a variety of contexts and situations, it is variously named as a communication theory, a critical theory, a practical theory or a transformation theory. Barnett and I realized that, for us, CMM is not a theory at all but rather a way of seeing and living and being in the world. We coined the phrase, "using CMM as a spiritual practice" as a placeholder for our own experience of our minds and hearts expanding as we used its concepts, tools, and models.

As you've read the previous paragraph, I hope one of your take-aways is that CMM is not one thing. If you are with people who use it you may find there are as many variations on its uses as there are users. Hopefully this will free you from thinking that there is a "right way" to use CMM. Having said that, here is how Barnett and I think about CMM: it begins with one's view of "communication" and what we "see" as a result. Barnett coined the term "taking the communication perspective" as a way of naming this other view of communication.

Taking the Communication Perspective

The other night I watched a fascinating program about a man who swims unimpeded with great white sharks. He talked about how he has learned to understand them through observation; his conclusion—we need not fear them. And to prove his point, he swims with them! As I was watching the underwater dance between this man and the sharks, I imagined the sharks being quite aware of their surroundings—the man, the camera he was holding in front of him, the other fish, and the boat above them. I also imagined the sharks being *unaware* of the water that they were swimming in because of its ubiquitous nature. I flashed to human communication; from birth to death we are swimming in patterns of communication. And for us, these patterns are ubiquitous and mostly out of awareness because we are never not engaged in them. We feel the *consequences* of our communicating, just as sharks experience the consequences of polluted or healthy oceanic waters, but we don't "see" the patterns themselves.

Many of our communication patterns are "polluted." They elicit expressions of destructive anger, suspicion, fear, to name a few, which makes compassion, openness and trust far more difficult to achieve.

Why don't we "see" communication as material and substantive? One answer to this question is that we have been raised and trained not to see it. I'd like to pause and do a thought experiment: You have been asked to provide a definition of communication for dictionary.com. What is your definition of communication?

If you are like most of us, your definition will say something like this: *Communication is the exchange of ideas and information. It can be verbal or nonverbal and it can occur in writing, in speech, in person, or in an on-line medium.* This is a definition, or something like this, that you will find in virtually every dictionary. I have also asked my college students during the past decade to define communication; without exception they offer a version similar to the one that you have just read.

About 400 years ago, two extremely influential philosophers, John Locke and David Hume, asserted that communication is a tool for the transmission of pure ideas: the ideas themselves were what mattered and not the vehicle for expressing and exchanging them.[2] That view of communicating took hold and, metaphorically, "went viral" because 400 years later, it is still how we understand and know communication. And because it is the lens through which we see and understand our communicating, we have developed a "learned incapacity" to see differently.

It's time to expand our vision and to take up a new lens. To go back to my previous metaphor, we need to become aware of "what we're swimming in" and how the water is affecting every aspect of our lives. To do this requires an "unlearning" and a "new learning" of what's happening every time we're communicating.

A NEW LENS FOR UNDERSTANDING COMMUNICATION BASED ON CMM: FOUR CLAIMS

The claims that I'm making about communication are these:

1. Communication is not just a tool for exchanging ideas and information. Rather, communication is "material." We can see it and feel it. It "makes" selves, relationships, organizations, communities, cultures, etc. This is what I have referred to as "taking the communication perspective;

2. Communication is a two-sided process involving stories that we and others tell to make sense of the world (CMM calls this making and managing meaning) and patterns of interaction or the back and forth flow of what people say and do (CMM calls this coordinating our actions together). This two-sided process is always occurring but the dance between them is complex and messy;

3. We get what we make. If your patterns of interaction contain destructive accusations and reactive anger you will most likely make a defensive relationship; if your patterns contain genuine questions and curiosity, you will have a better chance of making a more open relationship; and,

4. Get the pattern of communication right and the best possible things will happen.

I'd like to demonstrate these four claims through an extended example. The story I am about to tell you is true. It is also a story in which Barnett and I kept in mind the claims of communication and, consequently, acted quite differently than we might otherwise have acted.

When Barnett was diagnosed with an incurable form of cancer, none of the conversations we had with our family was easy. But the conversation that we were particularly dreading was with Barnett's dad. At the time, Pop was 91; he was living several States away from us in Tennessee with his partner, Lillian.

To give you some background, the type of communication that had developed between us over the years was quite predictable and superficial—conversations about the weather, various family members, visits to "nursing homes" as Pop calls them to sing gospel songs with the residents. Barnett told me the story of vividly remembering a conversation he and his dad had while Barnett was in college that has served as a metaphor for their relationship. Barnett was learning so many things that expanded and challenged the world that had been confined by his upbringing in Sebring, Florida and he found this expansion exhilarating. He came home from college and he couldn't wait to tell his dad about all of the things that he was learning. Pop listened for a few minutes and then said, "Son if I accept what you are telling me, it would undermine all that I've learned and done in my life." Barnett says that he was stunned and not skilled enough to continue the conversation. His take-away from that conversation was that he couldn't share his world in any significant way with his dad. Consequently, our conversations over the years have revolved around topics like "how are your tomato vines doing?" and "how are Lillian's shingles?...are they getting any better?" What Barnett has been able to do is to keep a respectful albeit superficial relationship, but it hasn't always been easy.

What we hoped would happen in our phone call to tell Pop about Barnett's cancer diagnosis was a deeper and more satisfying conversation. We had already spoken with Joy and Richard, Barnett's sister and brother-in-law and the four of us decided that it would be good if Joy and Richard were at the house with Pop when we called.

This is how the conversation went:

> Barnett: Hey Pop, how are you doing?

> Pop: Terrible, thank you! (This is his standard reply and he says it with lively energy and a twinkle in his eye.)

> Barnett and Kim: We inquire about how he and Lillian are doing, what the weather is like, and the visit they are having with Joy and Richard.

> Pop: I'm talking with Joy right now about my Will and I want to get back to my conversation with her soon. When are you coming to visit so I can tell you about the Will and my legal documents?

Barnett: We have some hard news to share that will make it impossible for us to visit in July like we had planned. "I have cancer, Dad."

Pop: Well, Son, I hope you're ready to meet your maker.

Barnett: Dad, I want you to know that I'm very secure with that.

Pop: Good, Son. I guess I'll see you on the other side.

Barnett: Dad, I don't want to tell you anymore than you want to hear, but if you have any questions, we are here to answer them.

Pop: No, Son. I don't have any questions. I've heard what I need to know. Do you want to talk with Joy or Richard?

Barnett: Sure, Dad, put Richard on the phone.

Richard tells us that Dad has picked up where he left off with Joy, talking about his Will and documents. We talk for a few more minutes and then Barnett asks Richard to tell Pop that he loves him. Richard says that this should be something that Dad hears from Barnett, so he puts Pop back on the line.

Barnett: I love you, Pop.

Pop: I love you too, Son. Goodbye.

Claims 1 and 2: Communication is a two-sided process of making and managing meaning and coordinating our actions…and what we say and do matters.

As you can imagine, this was a very hard conversation for Barnett and me. I was really angry at Pop's flippant responses and what felt like a lack of empathy. Barnett was also angry but I think mostly hurt that his Dad couldn't emotionally meet him in a way that a Son wishes his Father would do. If I had not been thinking about these first two claims about communication, I would have lashed out at Pop and said some hurtful things: "How can you be so cold? You are so cruel!" Although in the moment it may have felt good to me to say these things and get them off my chest, it would not have been useful for what Barnett was hoping might happen in the conversation. It most likely would have made a fight. So instead I held these feelings in tension with the kind of conversation that Barnett and I had hoped to make—one that was more meaningful than our typical conversations.

When we hung up, Barnett was sobbing. We talked about all of the relational connections that he and his dad don't have nor, most likely, ever will. He was sobbing at the sadness and the guilt he felt at having to tell his dad that he had cancer. He was sobbing because he wants a Father to meet him in his sadness and grief; instead, Barnett felt emotionally abused. I was crying too at how awful that conversation felt…and I expressed my anger to Barnett.

As Barnett and I were having this conversation, we began to talk about how easy it would be to dismiss Pop and label him as an unfeeling Father. Instead, we *deliberately* decided to talk about the various aspects of Pop that make him, like the rest of us, a complex person. We talked about Pop losing his first-born child and, later, his wife of over 50 years. We imagined the emotional scars that these experiences have left. We discussed how hard it must be to believe that your children will outlive you and then hear the news that this most likely won't happen. We talked about how cruel Pop's parents had been to him and how that pattern had continued with Pop. Enriching Pop was important for us in making and managing our stories of him. It made it possible for us to see him at the nexus of many difficult relationships and experiences in his life that have profoundly shaped him.

The conversation that Barnett and I had about Pop made it easier for both of us to see and treat him as a more complex person. It provided a crack in the door to act more compassionately than we otherwise would have. We also were clear that we would not initiate another conversation with Pop anytime soon.

Later in the week, Barnett received a letter from his dad:

> Dear Son:
>
> Here is my Father's Day gift! Son I am so proud of my son who made such an impression on this world. Made an impressive mark in college, won the national debate, on to Fort Worth, an MA and PhD….You have "impacted" thousands with knowledge, wisdom, and humor. May the Lord our Savior bless you here and say "well done" at the close your life.

Your Mother's and Father's benediction!

Pop

Wow! This is an amazing letter. Barnett's dad has never said these things to him...ever! It is an apology. It is an expression of love. It is an "opening" for a different kind of relationship. And what Barnett says and does next will "make" something as well. Barnett could respond by asking his dad why it's taken him this long to praise him? And although this is a "real and legitimate" question, Barnett also knows that asking a question like this will most likely elicit defensiveness. What Barnett wants to make is a closer relationship with his dad. So he chooses to write a letter back. Barnett's letter does two things simultaneously: it celebrates his love and gratitude for his dad while acknowledging Barnett's pain. The pain is heard differently, however, coming from Barnett at this point in their conversation and not earlier when, for example, Pop was so matter-of-fact on the phone.

For Father's Day

June 18, 2009

Dear Dad

Thanks for my Father's Day gift! It's hard for me to say how much your "benediction" means to me. I've always wanted you and Mom to be proud of me, and there is so much of me that I've learned from the two of you.

I'm content with the life I've led. I know that I've made a bunch of mistakes and if I could undo things that hurt other people, I would. But I've always tried to be true to myself, as poorly as I sometimes understood what that meant, and I'm happy with where I've come to. I love my life, my wife, my work, and my friends. I rode elephants in India and horses in Argentina, came face to face with a python in Malaysia, saw the green parrots at dawn in El Salvador, sailed along the coast in Norway, skied in Canada, swam with the dolphins in the Red Sea, watched the sun set in Sweden, played tennis in Colombia, France, Mexico and Denmark, and petted a wombat and counted kangaroos in Australia. I've traveled more widely than I ever expected to and have wonderful friends in all of the places that I've been to. For the most part, I've been able to spend my time working on the things that I would have done in my spare time. Pretty good!

I want to live longer. About five years ago, I had a cyst in my spine that crippled me until an operation set me free. I've been thinking about that in this way: have I used the "extra" five years well? I think so. And I'd like to have another five years of productive life.

Your approval is important. I know that I was often a trial and disappointment for you. Things that come to mind are my disinterest in fishing, hunting, and working in the yard! I know that you often didn't understand or approve of the things that interested me or decisions I made, and we've had some rough times. I am so happy that we've moved beyond them and can be as close as we are.

I don't know why I wasn't more of the son that you wanted or expected. I remember Mom asking me once "Son, where did you come from?" When I was growing up, you and Mom were pretty much estranged from your parents, from the Barnetts, and certainly from the Bassetts, so I never was deeply enmeshed in our extended family. But there was a lot of unspoken history from those family relations that I only vaguely sensed or learned about later. I remember the story you told me about how your parents were disappointed that you didn't marry ... (I've forgotten her name), and you only learned about that years later. As I recall, you said "why didn't you tell me?" But one of the lessons that I learned from you and Mom was to be true to myself rather than to reproduce the patterns of your parents. You and Mom made a life together despite your parents' objections. I learned from that. In many ways, my own need to be independent and to live a life that explored its own possibilities is a more valid imitation of you than if I had loved to shoot squirrels from the tree.

And I also learned other things from you. You are such a bundle of contradictions (as we all are). You often talk harshly, criticizing other people for being different from you or not acting in ways that you approve. AND, despite how you speak, you display kindness in a thousand other ways. I remember your acts of kindness to Pete (I never did know his last name). I remember how you hunted down the police department in Savannah so that you could pay the ten cents for the broken parking meter. I know how you have "helped" many people all through your life ... Iva; Rosie Whitwer (do I spell that correctly?) and more. I remember driving to the trailer park in ... was it Lakeland? ... to visit a lonely lady whom we used to live next to. These lessons have been important to me.

And Mom. Bless her heart, I'm so sorry that I never got to
know her as an adult, not just "Mom." But she set such an
example of caring for others. I think it hard to exaggerate
how much of the "me-at-my-best" is my attempt to imitate
her. Or please her. I wish she could have known the great-
grandchildren, and have known Kim – she would have liked
them so much.

So if I've become a person that you can approve of, you
and Mom have only yourselves to blame! The most precious
words I can say are:

Thanks, Dad.

Barnett

Two weeks later, Barnett got a note on floral stationery from
his dad.

The hand-written message says only this: "A bowl of flowers for
my beloved son."

Our conversations with Pop occurred with greater frequency
after the exchange of these letters.   A few months later we
received a letter from Dad on the same stationery with the floral
background. The letter read:

Dear Son and Kim—my last bouquet, thought I'd send it
to two very important loved ones. We have progressed far
beyond the days of disappointment we sometimes went thru.
I only wish Ethlene could have known Kim….

I love you,

Pop

I use this extended example because it is a transformational
relationship in the making. And it begs the question, "how did
that happen?" No doubt there are many reasons and explanations
as to why this happened as it did. One explanation was that
a health crisis occurred that shook us out of our complacency.
Yes, the crisis occurred so perhaps that was the crack in the door.
A second explanation was that Barnett and I took seriously the
notion that every conversation is "making" something; what we
wanted to make was greater closeness between ourselves and
Pop. That meant that we didn't say and do things during our
initial call with Pop. For example, we didn't tell Pop any more
than he wanted to know about Barnett's cancer diagnosis; we

didn't lash out in our anger and hurt; Barnett didn't close down emotionally although he wanted to—instead he ended their conversation by expressing his love for his Dad. These ways of being with Pop left an opening for something better to happen, leaving the crack in the door a bit wider. And thankfully, Pop's next conversational turn of the letter opened the door even more for Barnett to eventually express a full range of thoughts and emotions about his Father, to his Father.

If you take the first two claims seriously that the stories we tell and the ways that we coordinate with each other are always making something, then it is incumbent upon us to develop the mindfulness to act with greater wisdom and compassion in the moment. Our years of practice made it possible for Barnett and me to stay open to Pop even in profound disappointment and anger, and to remember that Pop, like all of us, is much more complex than the labels of "cold, uncaring Father" that we felt during our phone call with him.

Looking for Bifurcation Points as we are Engaging with Others

Every conversation of which we are a part has what CMM calls "bifurcation points"; that is, places in the conversation where what happens next will affect the unfolding pattern of interaction and take it in a different direction. A clear bifurcation point occurred when Pop's first response to the news of Barnett's cancer was that he hoped Barnett was ready to meet his Maker. Had we not responded mindfully into the conversational fork in the road, the conversation could have gone like this:

> Barnett: We have some hard news to share that will make it impossible for us to visit in July like we had planned. "I have cancer, Dad."

> Pop: Well, Son, I hope you're ready to meet your Maker.

> Kim: What a cold thing to say!! Don't you have the decency to feel the pain that your son feels?

> Pop: And don't you love the Lord? If you did you'd know that there's nothing more important than meeting your Maker?

> Kim: Jesus showed more compassion for so-called sinners than you're showing to your own son…. You call yourself a Christian?

You see where this conversation is going? And everything that Pop and I have said in this alternative exchange is true from our own perspectives. But saying these things at this point in the conversation will most likely make hard feelings and a fight. And the farther we get into this kind of conversational pattern, the easier it is to "feel compelled" to say and do things that we will later regret. So it's useful to keep in mind the notion that what you say and do "next" is important to the unfolding dynamic of the conversation.

This isn't rocket science, but it requires us to be aware of the unfolding pattern and "my part" in making the pattern. It requires that we think about what we "want to make" in the interaction (i.e., Barnett and I wanted to make a closer relationship with Pop), what is actually getting made in our moment by moment exchanges (i.e., I want to make more openness but when he just made that accusation, I reacted by retaliating and now we've made a fight), and ways to help make a better situation (i.e., I realize my part in making this fight; I'm going to acknowledge my part and ask if we can try again).

Having said that, there is no guarantee that your desire to make something specific will result in just what you hoped for. You are always part of an "unfolding pattern" so "your turn" contributes to but is only part of what gets made. For example, Barnett's long letter back to Pop could have gone without a response. Had that happened, our experience would have been closer to "polite fence mending" after an uncomfortable phone call rather than the compassionate exchange of deep love, acceptance, and forgiveness that actually occurred. That said, we can always influence "the possibility for something better" and with that, our intentions to make something can often take root and influence others' next turn.

I hope the previous example helps you to see the consequential nature and the two-sided process of communication in action. Now put the previous example in the context of **billions** of such exchanges that occur throughout our lifetime. This is what we're "swimming in" and why we need to do our part to make the "healthiest oceans" possible.

Claims 3 and 4: We get what we make and get the pattern right and the best possible things will happen

I'd like to turn now to the third and fourth claims: 3. We get what we make. If your patterns of interaction contain destructive accusations and reactive anger you will most likely make a defensive relationship; if your patterns contain genuine questions and curiosity, you will have a better chance of making a more open relationship; and, 4. Get the pattern of communication right and the best possible things will happen.

The third claim "you get what you make" calls attention to the fact that communicating makes "real" things:

It makes certain kinds of selves, including different bodily sensations. Think about the self you become, including what is happening in your body, when you are in an unproductive angry exchange with someone versus the self that is elicited when you and another are listening deeply to each other even if the conversation is difficult;

It makes relationships. Every relationship has a certain energy and that energy comes from the ways that people are relating, or not, with each other; and,

It makes "cultures"; family cultures, organizational cultures, community cultures, religious cultures, classroom cultures etc. Cultures get made when we engage in similar communication patterns over and over again.

My daughter is an elementary school substitute teacher. When she walks in the classroom and begins interacting with the children, she quickly learns what kind of culture and environment the primary teacher has created. The children are *embodying* the communication patterns that have become acceptable or unacceptable. She tells me about some classroom cultures in which the kids follow instructions and they do what she asks. Other cultures are more chaotic with kids telling each other to shut up, getting in and out of their seats, and not following her instructions. Interestingly, the classroom cultures with the "easiest" children are the ones in which the teacher has left the most detailed instructions for my daughter. If a teacher creates and abides by clear standards for classroom behavior, the kids know what to do and they act into that culture. This embodiment applies to all of the groups to which we belong.

The repetitive patterns of communication are out of awareness, because we're not trained to think about or notice patterns. But their effects are "real" and we feel/experience them daily.

Which leads to the fourth claim: get the pattern of communication right and the best possible things will happen. When I say "get the pattern right" I mean in a single conversation as well as conversations that occur over time.

With people with whom we have on-going interactions, it's not unusual to solidify certain ways of communicating and being together. It's like this—there is a dirt road close to my house that my dog Luke and I walk on everyday. This road is also traveled by big cement trucks. When it rains and the trucks drive on the road, they leave grooves in the road. This has happened so much that there are now permanent grooves in the road. So now, rain or shine, when the trucks drive down this road, the tires will find their way into the grooves.

Think of conversations you have had with people that have the quality of a "groove." The pattern has solidified to the point of accurately predicting how the conversation will unfold if you bring up topic X. A friend of mine, for example, tells me that she will not talk with her daughter about politics because she knows that it will lead to a fight. She doesn't want to make a fight, but she doesn't know how to interact with her daughter without the "pattern" that they have developed over the years "taking over." Calcified patterns can take on a life of their own— we feel "compelled" to respond in a particular way, as does our partner, and before you know it the pattern has repeated itself yet again! CMM has called these "unwanted repetitive patterns" (URPs).

Our pattern with Pop over the years was of superficial conversations. We made that pattern because of previous attempts that Barnett had made to make his world available to Pop and Pop's refusal to enter that world. So Barnett stopped trying to make something different, until his cancer diagnosis. And then he tried again. This time, he was more skilled at thinking about what he hoped to make with Pop. When Pop said some hurtful things, Barnett didn't respond like he had done many years in the past. He allowed Pop's comments to remain unchallenged (at least in that moment) believing that there was a better chance of making openness if Barnett remained open.

Barnett left the door open for a more compassionate next turn by telling his dad that he loved him. And Pop responded to this turn with a beautiful, first of its kind, letter.

If we "get the pattern right" we have the best chance of good things happening. What do I mean by getting the pattern right? In most cases, anything we can do to help increase compassion, openness, trust, and respect, for example, will help create better things—better selves, better relationships, better decisions, and better ongoing patterns. We all know what it feels like to be heard, to be respected despite different views, to engage in spirited discussions in which curiosity is a guiding principle, and to reach a deeper and richer understanding of an issue and other people because of the quality and the presence of the participants. The more we can approximate these kinds of interactions, the better our social worlds. It's also important that you do not hear me saying that getting the pattern right means minimizing differences. Neither does getting the pattern right mean that the full range of our human emotions and experiences cannot or should not be expressed (Recall Barnett's letter to his Dad in which he said that Pop often talks harshly and unfairly criticizes others.). But the timing of our comments and the way that we say them make all the difference in the unfolding interaction.

As I said earlier, this isn't rocket science. We know these things intuitively and we certainly feel and carry them in our body. We also know that what I'm describing doesn't just happen. We need to practice, and practice, and practice some more, and continue practicing until we have taken our last breath.

John Dewey in 1891 understood the importance of our actions in making better social worlds:

> "In a word, a man has not to do Justice and Love and Truth; he has to do justly and truly and lovingly. And this means that he has to respond to the actual relations in which he finds himself. To do truly is to regard the whole situation as far as one sees it, and to see it as far as one can; to do justly is to give a fit and impartial regard to each member of this situation, according to its place in the system; to do lovingly is to make the whole situation one's own, not dividing into parts of which one is a warm meum and the other a cold tuum."[3]

This last sentence is similar to the last sentence of Pema Chodron's earlier quote, "...it's an experience that's expansive enough to include all that arises."

Not only a voice from the past, but two voices from the present looking into the future are talking about the importance of coordinating our actions and making and managing our meanings without having heard of CMM. These are prominent futurists from Intel and here's what they are saying:

> "Let's get one thing straight: the future is not set. The future is not some fixed point just over the horizon that we are all helplessly hurtling towards. No, we are not powerless. The future is not written. *The future is made every day by the actions of people.*" –Brian David Johnson, *The Tomorrow Project Anthology (2011)*

> "I guess the way you change the future is to change people's narrative. Change the story people have imagined the future will be. Change that and you change the future. Everything else is far too complicated and out of a single person's control—but just change the story we tell ourselves about the future and you change the future itself." – Cory Doctorow, *The Tomorrow Project Anthology (2011)*

So what stories will we tell and what persons will we be... individually and together? May the social DNA of our communicating be based on mindfulness of its ubiquitous nature and the role that each of us play in creating, shaping, and maintaining patterns that will help the planet and every living thing on it to thrive. This is a future that, should we live in to, will make more loving and compassionate selves, relationships, and cultures.

4

Mindfulness of Our Social Worlds

FOUR PATHS TO SOCIAL ENLIGHTENMENT

It is one thing to talk about the communication perspective (looking *at* communication and not *through* it) and it is another to live it. Among other things, making this shift requires mindfulness. By mindfulness I mean a keen awareness of the ways that our social worlds (selves, relationships, families, organizations, communities…) get made one conversation at a time. I also mean awareness of the part that each of us plays through our words and actions in helping to make these social worlds. And lastly, I'm thinking of mindfulness as the ability to discern ways of acting in the moment in difficult situations to help make that situation a better one for the participants involved.

With respect to the Buddha, here are Four Paths to Enlightenment about Social Worlds that are grounded in mindfulness of taking the communication perspective. I am also using the language of CMM as I talk about mindfulness of coordinating our actions with others and make and manage meaning. These four paths will be fleshed out in Section 2 of this book through actual practices and exercises.

1.   Mindful of yourself:

   •   What *you* say and do matters

   •   Thoughts affect actions

   •   Actions make our social worlds

   •   You become what you do

   •   Your heart and mind will grow as you practice compassion

   •   Practice M/mystery as a lens for developing greater compassion for "you"

2. Mindful of what CMM calls "making/managing meanings" through the stories we tell:

- Stories grow out of our experiences and we are shaped by them

- All stories are local, incomplete and unfinished

- Curiosity deepens appreciation for the complexity of stories

- Deep listening fosters the exploration of the fuller story

- The manner of storytelling affects the willingness of others to stay open and curious

- Practice M/mystery as a lens for developing greater compassion for the stories of others that are antithetical to your stories

3. Mindful of what CMM calls "coordinating with others" or, said differently, the ways that a conversation unfolds over time:

- All conversations have multiple turns (you say something, I respond to what you've said, you respond to what I've said…and if the relationship is an established one we will bring in "the history of what we've said and done….")

- Each turn is a response to something and it elicits a response

- Every turn opens up or closes down possibilities

- The quality of our conversations affect selves, relationships, and our social worlds

- We get what we make

- Practice M/mystery as a lens for developing compassion and awe and wonder for the complexity of the coordinated dances we engage in moment by moment

4. Mindful of what CMM calls "making better social worlds":

    ·   Think in terms of patterns and relationships

    ·   Recognize your part in making the patterns of which you are a part

    ·   Develop habits and skills that foster mindfulness of various perspectives

    ·   Develop habits and skills that foster curiosity and compassion

    ·   Practice M/mystery as a lens for developing compassion, humility, and awe and wonder for the complexity of our social worlds

OK, I can imagine some of your saying "sounds like a useful bulleted list. But how do you realistically do it and live it?" One answer is to use the CMM models as a form of "mindfulness practice." All of the models are doing similar things; they are calling attention to various aspects of our social worlds and helping us to become more aware of the co-evolutionary process of our stories and actions in making those worlds.

MINDFULNESS OF OUR SOCIAL WORLDS: USING CMM MODELS

I'm going to briefly introduce the models of CMM and refer back to the exchange Barnett and I had with Pop to illuminate how we used these models to guide our actions. As I'm describing the use of the models in helping us know how to "go on" in our conversation with Pop, keep in mind that we've been using these for years in our daily lives. Also, keep in mind that in our conversations with Pop, we are bringing the fullness of ourselves into the moment. Among other things, this means that we are experiencing a full range of emotions and feelings. As you're reading the descriptions, if you are still confused don't worry. In Section 2 of this handbook I'll provide more detailed instructions about how to use these models in practice.

Daisy Model: The Daisy Model is a way of depicting that events in our social worlds are deeply textured and a situation always involves multiple participants and myriad conversations (most of which are not physically present but nonetheless can be quite influential). These networks of people and conversations can be internalized voices, the voices of others, the voices of people no longer physically alive but very much present, etc. To use the model, the center of the daisy would describe the situation or person under consideration. Each petal would represent a different person, organization, cluster of organizations, or stories impacting the situation. One can then begin to tease out the connections among the petals, describe individuals or organizations who are strongest, weakest, silent, etc. The goal is to better understand the larger system of which the event and participants are a part and to experience mystery, compassion, and humility about the complexity of our social worlds.

DAISY

The Daisy model can be used in a systematic way by focusing on each petal and teasing out the relationships among petals, etc. The model can also be used briefly and in the moment as a way of reminding yourself that the person in front of you is much more complex than your experience of her in the moment.

Without actually drawing a daisy, Barnett and I used the model right after we had our difficult conversation with Pop. Recall that I told you that our anger and hurt were making it easy for us to label Pop as an uncaring, unsupportive, and cruel Father, period and exclamation point!! But we know that, like all of us, he is more complex than that. The Daisy model helped us to practice the "naming" of the other aspects of Pop. Our conversation helped us remember that Pop lost his first-born child when she was less than a year old and, later, his wife of over 50 years. We imagined the emotional scars that these experiences have left. We discussed how hard it must be to believe that your children will outlive you and then hear the news that this most likely won't happen. In Pop's case it means that he has outlived two of his three children. We were then reminded that Pop has outlived most of his siblings (and he was the firstborn in his family of 7 children). We talked about how cruel Pop's parents had been to him even thought he was a dutiful son.

Enriching Pop was important for us in making and managing our stories of him. It made it possible for us to see him at the nexus of many difficult relationships and experiences in his life that have profoundly shaped him. Doing this helped me put my anger and my father-in-law into a larger framework.

Hierarchy Model of Meanings/Stories: All conversations occur in contexts. The Hierarchy Model is designed to help participants understand the highest contexts out of which they and others are acting. When two or more participants see, understand, and articulate quite different stories about a situation, they may be operating out of different higher-level contexts. All events include several types of contexts (i.e., the actual episode or situation, one's sense of self, the importance of the relationship, the cultural stories and cultural constraints, etc.). Exploring and naming one's own and other participants' higher level contexts can be extremely helpful in understanding the different frames and forces that are contributing to the unfolding interactional pattern.

My friend Philip found the use of the hierarchy model helpful in understanding the dynamics between him and his brother when they play tennis. His brother is a fierce competitor and he really likes to win. The episode of the tennis match is his highest context. Occasionally, Philip will play better than his brother. Philip finds, however, that when he's too close to winning he backs off and softens up a bit. As he puzzled over this he realized that the relationship with his brother and having a good time was more important than winning; in the game of tennis, playing with his brother is more important than winning. Consequently, he backs off if he's ahead.

Philip's hierarchy of meaning looks like this:

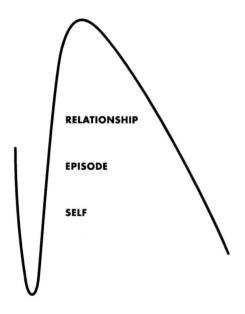

RELATIONSHIP

EPISODE

SELF

Going back to my story about Pop, if I'm consciously making mystery my highest-level context and story while I'm talking to Pop, I will suspend my snap judgments and remember that our social worlds are deeply textured and complex as are the people in them. This allows me to hold my anger with more of an open hand rather than a closed fist. If self is my highest context and story as I'm talking to Pop, I'll be more focused on what I need and want throughout the interaction.

What actually happened is that Barnett and I were privileging "relationship" as our highest-level story of what we wanted to be guided by as we spoke with Pop. We also talked about this explicitly before the conversation. This meant that we focused on what we could say or do next to help keep the relationship open. Interestingly, it was after our painful conversation and our use of the Daisy model that my highest-level story shifted from relationship to mystery. The use of the Daisy model focused our attention on some of the very difficult experiences Pop has had around death and loss, and that elicited a profound sense of humility and compassion from both of us.

The Serpentine Model: The Serpentine Model is a way of describing a sequence of actions through time and the ways that each act elicits a particular response from the participants. This model can also be used in conjunction with the Hierarchy Model to help identify the highest levels of context and/or to identify "forces" or the feeling that occurs in many conversations that I *must* or I *can't* respond in this way. These conversational forces often compel people to say and do things that they know will make matters worse but they just "can't help it." The model is useful in helping people explore the stories that guide actions, what those actions elicit from others, and what is getting made as a result.   The model can be used by several people at once (the group can reconstruct a difficult conversation and work together to understand why it unfolded as it did) or by an individual. The model can also be used "after the fact" to understand what went wrong or in the moment to act as wisely as possible into your "next conversational turn."

Since Barnett and I have used CMM models for many years, we used the serpentine to think about the conversation *before* we had it and then in real time throughout the conversation.   Before the conversation began, we talked about what we thought was important for this conversation to go well.   One of our conclusions was that we didn't want Pop to hear about Barnett's cancer diagnosis without a close family member being with him. So we contacted Barnett's sister and brother-in-law and made arrangements for them to be at the house when we called. In our minds, this was the "first turn" in our conversation with Pop.

> *Turn #1:* Creating the conditions for Pop to have family support during and after our phone call.
>
> During the actual phone call, we didn't want to begin with bad news. We thought that it was important for us to hear how Pop is doing before we launch into such hard news.
>
> *Turn #2:* We begin the conversation by asking Dad how he is. We inquire about how he and Lillian are doing, what the weather is like, and the visit they are having with Joy and Richard. His dad is a bit short, as he has been in the middle of talking to Joy about his Will and all of the legal documents that he has told us both about on more than a few occasions; he is, after all, 91. So he quickly turns the conversation to his question of when we will be coming to visit him so he can tell us about these documents and his wishes should something happen to him.
>
> *Turn #3:* Barnett tells him that we have some hard news to share that will make it impossible for us to visit in July like we had planned. "I have cancer, Dad."
>
> *Turn #4:* Pop's immediate response: "Well, Son, I hope you're ready to meet your maker."

Wow! A huge fork in the road (CMM's term is bifurcation point)! I am so angry at Pop for his insensitivity. I want to say, "what a terrible thing to say!...can't you meet your son in his pain?" And I also have a very strong impulse to want to protect Barnett from Pop's insensitive comments. But I am also aware that this next turn is very important for the unfolding dynamic that will occur. So I remain quiet.

> *Turn #5:* Barnett speaks, "Dad, I want you to know that I'm very secure with that."
>
> *Turn #6:* " Good, Son. I guess I'll see you on the other side."

Again, another huge bifurcation point. These platitudes are the last thing we need or want to hear right now. My anger is increasing and seeing Barnett's face I know his sadness is intensifying. But we continue to think about the "next turn" and what we might say or do to help keep the relationship as open as possible.

Turn #7: Barnett intervenes again by inviting Pop to ask us questions. "Dad, I don't want to tell you anymore than you want to hear, but if you have any questions, we are here to answer them."

Turn #8: "No, Son. I don't have any questions. I've heard what I need to know. Do you want to talk with Joy or Richard?"

Another bifurcation point! As I look at Barnett's face, I now see anger. However, he chooses not to express this. Instead he says...

Turn #10: "Sure, Dad, put Richard on the phone."

Turn #10: Richard tells us that Dad has picked up where he left off with Joy, talking about his Will and documents. We talk for a few more minutes and then Barnett asks Richard to tell Pop that he loves him. Richard says that this should be something that Dad hears from Barnett, so he puts Pop back on the line.

Barnett is sobbing now and I imagine that he is experiencing the relational connections that he and his dad don't have nor, most likely, ever will. I also imagine that he is sobbing at feeling emotionally abandoned by his Dad. But because he is able to hold these feelings and experiences in a larger context of wanting to make something different with his dad, his last conversational turn is an affirmation of a future possibility.

Turn #11: He ends by simply saying, "Dad, I love you."

Turn #12: "I love you too, Son. Goodbye."

Among other things, this conversation was possible for us because we had a model to help us think about "what will we do next?" to help make a more satisfying conversation. And we are not just "in our heads." We both felt intense anger and sadness and Barnett felt emotionally abandoned by his dad. But we held these emotions and experiences in a broader context of the unfinished and unfolding social world we were making with Pop.

LUUUUTT Model: LUUUUTT is an acronym for 1) stories **L**ived; 2) **U**nknown stories, 3) **U**ntold Stories, 4) **U**nheard stories, 5)

Untellable stories; 6) Stories Told, and 7) storyTelling. This model is used to explore the gaps between the lived and told stories, stories that are privileged, stories that are underdeveloped or eerily silent, and the manner of story telling. The model is used to enrich and expand the stories you and others tell by helping us move from slogans and anecdotes to full stories. To the extent that we are telling fuller stories, we are able to live with complexity and greater compassion. We also become more mindful of the way that we tell our stories and its effects on others.

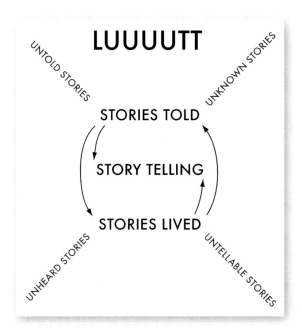

Pop's lived and told story is the "salvation story" of Christianity. His Christian faith is the lens through which he views the world and it was front and center when we talked with him about Barnett's cancer diagnosis. And although I was angry and offended by his insensitive remarks, I also realized, when I took a step back from the situation, that his salvation story may make it possible for Pop to know how to "go on" in the face of the terrible news of his son's terminal illness. As Barnett and I used the Daisy model to enrich Pop, it also helped me to begin to think about the untold and untellable stories of losing his first child, his wife, and all but two of his siblings. I also wondered about unknown stories of any crises of faith that may play into his being "over zealous" in his religious comments. I was also aware that his "manner of speaking" throughout the conversation of such flippant responses might be a coping mechanism that wouldn't allow him to feel untellable stories that are too painful to bear.

The point of using the LUUUUTT model is not to "find the correct story" or "the correct interpretation" as much as enlarging your awareness of how complex our social worlds are. Every interaction carries the seeds of past interactions and experiences. The more aware we are of the complexity of our social worlds, the greater our capacity for holding frustrating situations and people more compassionately.

As I said earlier, there is no one correct way to use the CMM models. Think of them as a scaffold to help you and others become more mindful of stories, of actions, and of the social worlds that we are creating together.

You might ask, "what is this increased awareness in service of?" In the case of Pop, it's in service of helping to make a more meaningful relationship. And fortunately, when Barnett died our relationship with Pop had been transformed into a tender and compassionate embrace. On a larger scale, this takes us back to the claim I made at the beginning of this handbook: we are living in a historical epoch in which the humanness expressed in people like Jesus and the Buddhist monk is essential for our survival. A predominant form of communication throughout the world continues to be "ethnocentric;" I'm right and you're wrong; either/or and black/white thinking. We know all too well that these patterns make more of the same. If we become skilled enough to consistently look "at" communication and not "through" it and use the tools and models of CMM to increase mindfulness, we are on the road to becoming virtuosos of our social worlds, making subtle and keen distinctions about unfolding patterns of communication and acting wisely in the moment into situations where what we say and do next will make a difference. And, paradoxically, if we can do this while keeping Mystery the highest level of context, our evolutionary journey will not be a burden to bear but a journey into the mystery of compassion and love, wherever we are in the process. So let us commit ourselves to a next level of personal and social evolution that "normalizes" on a daily basis the enactment of compassion.

2

SECTION 2: PRACTICES

5

An Introduction to the Practices

I realize the first section has covered a lot of ground, so let me briefly summarize what I am attempting to say:

- We are living in an unprecedented historical period in which those of us on the planet are inextricably interconnected economically, socially, and technologically in ways we have never been…and we also have the ability to destroy life as we know it;

- These two realities make the way we co-construct our humanness very important;

- At this time in history it is also imperative that we understand the role of communication in *making* our social worlds;

- When we really "know from the inside" the ways that our communication make real things such as selves, relationships, families and communities we are more sensitive to the importance of acting with humility and compassion;

- We know it is possible to live a life characterized by compassion because of role models like Jesus, the Dalai Lama, Aung San Suu Kyi, Thich Nhat Hanh, to name a few. This way of being in the world should not be seen as the province of saints and sages; it is possible for all of us;

- This way of being *does not mean* that we don't experience an entire range of emotions. It *does mean* that we hold all of these emotions as compassionately as we can and act as wisely as we are able;

- This level of mindfulness and social virtuosity occurs through a life-long and on-going commitment to effective sets of practices

- Using the tools and models of CMM is *one form* of practice;

- As we become more developed in our practice, our minds will expand and our hearts will grow;

- Our work of personal and social evolution is knowing that, through the lens of Mystery, every stage of development is held in a compassionate and loving embrace;

- Wherever you are in your personal evolutionary journey, it's OK. Compassionately hold and love yourself in this moment and beyond. This bulleted statement is seen through the lens of Mystery: the paradox is that the journey and the destination are one...so love it all!

I am now feeling the need to say a bit more about mystery. You may have noticed that I am spelling it in two ways: one is with a Capital M and the other is lower case m. The experiences I described in my dream refer to big M Mystery; the bulleted list about the four paths to social enlightenment includes both spellings of mystery; and, the bulleted list just above this paragraph includes both references to M/mystery. When Barnett and I were extending CMM to a spiritual practice, this was our first attempt at differentiating two experiences of mystery. We did this by using upper and lower case letters to distinguish Big M Mystery from little m mystery.

Our thought at the time was that Big M Mystery points to ineffability and to awe and wonder. It is the recognition that there are some things that can never be said adequately or that render you speechless—when you look at a beautiful sunset over the ocean, or you can see the Milky Way in the Arizona night sky for example, or you are witnessing the fierce and destructive power of a storm, ineffability, awe, and wonder come unbidden. It is also the recognition that whatever we may try to say about these things, there is always more that can be said...and it will never be enough! This view of Mystery is consistent with the ideas expressed in Barnett's 1989 book, *Communication and the Human Condition*. Big M Mystery is also consistent with the *Powers of 10* book, video and thought experiment.[4] Imagine a couple picnicking in Grant Park in Chicago. You are looking at the couple from a few feet away. The book then moves outward by powers of 10 with the couple always at the focal point. By the sixth frame we see planet earth floating in space. Six more frames and we are well out of our solar system and into deep space. One unmistakable take away is that the universe is BIG and whatever we might say about it there is always something more that can be said. And sometimes the only appropriate response is silence...and awe and wonder at the sheer immensity of it all. For me, Powers of 10 is also an exercise of embracing the paradox of Big M Mystery. The couple in Grant Park are enjoying a day together *that matters*, while a baby is being born in New Zealand and a woman is dying in combat in Afghanistan... on a tiny planet hurtling through space amidst trillions and trillions of galaxies in a universe that we will *never* come close to wrapping our minds around and will one day be no more. All of these realities are joined in holy matrimony.

Little m mystery is the mystery of our social worlds. It's the recognition that our social worlds are infinitely complex, that we are infinitely complex, and anything we might say about one's self, others, or our social worlds will always be incomplete and partial. It is the awe and wonder of our human relationships. Both of these experiences of mystery lead to a profound sense of humility...of, among other things, what we don't know.

At the time we were making these distinctions, Barnett and I saw big M Mystery in the context of the natural world and little m mystery in the context of our social worlds. I now think big M Mystery infuses our social worlds as well. What I'm finding in my own practice of using the lens of little m mystery in my social worlds is that when I keep at it, especially in very challenging situations, a transformational shift occurs that I didn't think was possible. One way of naming the embodied experience of this shift is that love and compassion show up. It is as if a "something much bigger than me" is meeting the "me that is practicing mystery" and that moment transforms into a Big M Mystery experience. I am *always* surprised when it happens and I'm always aware that something larger than me is a work. I'm at the edge of my own learning in attempting to articulate this, so bear with me. At the moment, one distinction I'm making about the two experiences of mystery is that most of the practices in this section invoke small m mystery. Stay with the practices and at some point the experience of Big M Mystery occurs.

One of the last workshops Barnett and I did together was in London sponsored by the Institute of Family Therapy and our dear friend Barbara McKay. The workshop was about using CMM as a spiritual practice. I don't remember the context in which this statement occurred, but someone used a phrase that I think is profoundly helpful. The phrase is: *Minding the Gap.* Minding the gap is a phrase that you'll find in Britain on the doors of subway cars reminding people not to fall into the gap between the car and the platform. I would like to explore this metaphor as a way of introducing the CMM practices. Before you read on, I encourage you to sit with the phrase for a moment and see what emerges for you.

As a metaphor and with the emphasis on *gap*, minding the gap makes me think of the space between things. In music, the untrained ear may tend to focus on the notes. But it's the spaces between the notes that affect the pace, the mood and the feel of the music. Additionally, it is in the gap between things that something new can emerge. Think about a continuous highway. There are no opportunities to circle around or make a left or right turn; there is only one direction you can go. Now think of that same highway with gaps that are large enough to make other choices about where to possibly travel. In our social worlds, think of an "incessant talker" who doesn't create gaps for others to join in. What type of relationship is possible? And, how about the incessant doer who fills the day with activity? What kinds of openings are possible? In a poem I wrote about ants making their way to the top of a barrel cactus, I end by saying, "look for the *spaces* between the obstacles. Walk there."

Gaps provide the ability for something new to emerge.

And now I shift to the first part of the metaphor, *minding*. Now imagine I'm back on the highway with gaps in the road that make it possible for me to explore new and different directions. But I'm listening to music and daydreaming about last night's party and, consequently, I'm completely unaware of the spaces in the road that will allow something new to happen. I'm singing along with the music blaring from my car stereo but I'm also not thinking about the lyrics, or paying attention to the spaces between the words, to what's not being said in this song. I'm on "auto-pilot". Of course our attention is always directed somewhere. So the question becomes to what are we paying attention and what quality of mind are we bringing to the situation.

Gaps need awareness to be fruitful.

Among other things, individual and social evolution requires a quality of attention. Every conversation (within ourselves and between people) becomes an opportunity to mind the gap: to *be aware of the spaces* that provide openings for us to travel down this road of a social world as opposed to that one…or to, with awe and wonder, explore several roads that lead in opposite directions.

The practices in this section are designed to increase your awareness of the spaces, openings, and possibilities for creating greater love and compassion for you and others. Each chapter will focus on a different aspect of our social worlds. Chapter 6 is devoted to practices to increase "mindfulness of self." Chapter 7 guides you through practices designed to increase your "mindfulness of the stories you tell and of the ways that you make and manage meaning." Chapter 8 turns to practices of coordination or the dance that we do with others in every conversation. The last chapter focuses your attention on practices that can help make better social worlds.

6

Mindfulness of Self

The First Set of Practices: Mindfulness of Self

Among other things, practicing mindfulness of self is to remember that:

- What *you* say and do matters

- Thoughts affect actions

- Actions make our social worlds

- You become what you do

- Your heart and mind will grow as you practice compassion

- Practice M/mystery as a lens for developing greater compassion for "you"

Your thoughts (about your self as well as about everything else in the world) matter and the stories you tell about your self will color every relationship in your life.

Last night I was watching a television program, *Dr. Oz*. Dr. Oz is a medical Doctor who provides tips for achieving a healthy lifestyle. Typically he focuses on exercise and diet. The theme of this particular episode however was the "self talk" that corrodes self-esteem and makes it easier to engage in unhealthy behavior. He conducted interview after interview with women who are abusing food, drugs and alcohol and who are experiencing relationship and health crises. And one by one, the women correlated their "self talk" about not being good enough, or smart enough, or skilled enough, or pretty enough... to their abusive and destructive behavior. What we say and do matters and our "self talk" does affect our actions.

The following 7 exercises are designed to help you think more systematically about the stories you tell about yourself ...pause... to appreciate the complexity of your social worlds ...pause...

and to hold yourself more compassionately and lovingly while supporting your growth and development.

EXERCISE #1: USING THE DAISY MODEL

TIME ALLOTMENT: 30 MINUTES

DESCRIPTION:

This first exercise is designed to enrich the stories you have about your self and of your life. It is also an exercise in mystery and of holding the many aspects of your life compassionately as you are mindfully aware of its complexities.

INSTRUCTIONS:

Put yourself at the center of the Daisy and begin to fill in the petals with the important people in your life and the various roles that you assume throughout a typical day. For example, my daisy would include various family members, friends, colleagues, my position in the CMM Institute, care giver for my aging parents, widow in transition... After the daisy is complete, consider the following prompts:

- **Looking over the entire daisy, love yourself for the complexity of your world and all that you are doing to juggle these multiple relationships and roles.**

- **Now spend time with each petal. As you focus on a petal be aware of:**

  - How does your body feel? Is it loose; tight; if tight, where do you notice the tightness? What is your body telling you?

  - What thoughts arise for you? Which of these are upfront and clear and which of them are cloudy and just taking shape?

  - What emotions arise? If you were to name the predominant emotions what would they be? What subtle feelings are present for you, but perhaps not fully felt yet?

  - Which voices do you hear? Which are the loudest and screaming for attention? Which voices are quiet or silent? Are there conversations you hear that are not part of your daisy but nonetheless affect you?

- **After you have spent time with each petal, I'd like you to look at all of the petals and draw your awareness to:**

  - Which petals are getting most of your attention? What arises for you as you are aware of these petals?

  - Which petals are crying out for more attention? What arises for you as you listen to these petals wanting more from you? Do you want to pay more attention to these petals?

  - Are there petals that are withering and are ready to drop off of your daisy? Can you imagine what your life would be like if you allowed the petal to fall away?

  - Are there petals that are missing from your daisy that you want to add? How will your life be different if this petal were a part of your life?

- Now celebrate again your life in its fullness and decide what you would like to do to keep your daisy as life giving and rich as possible.

INDIVIDUAL OR SMALL GROUP REFLECTIONS AFTER THE EXERCISE:

- As you did this exercise, what surprised you?

- What new insights are you gaining?

- How is this exercise affecting your stories of your self and of your life?

- What new actions are you thinking about taking?

- What was most challenging about the exercise?

- How might you think about this exercise in the context of "minding the gap"?

- How might you think about this exercise in the context of mystery (the awe and wonder and compassionate embrace about the complexity and diversity of your social world)?

Repeat this exercise as needed as one way of helping you sort through and story the various commitments, responsibilities, and people in your life…and of compassionately holding yourself in this complexity.

The next exercise is designed to help you think about your stories and experiences about the two types of mystery: Big M mystery and little m mystery. It is also meant to help you identify your current practices of both types of mystery. There are no right or wrong answers to these questions; remember that where ever you are in your thinking and practice of M/mystery, it's all OK!

Big M Mystery is the experience of awe and wonder of it all. At this very moment you and I are on an infinitesimally small blue globe rotating around a star that is part of a solar system in a galaxy hurtling through space among trillions of other galaxies. And while all of this is going on, two people in love are delighting in each other, a small child is discovering the sand and ocean water for the first time, the cycle of life is playing out in the wild savannah, a drought is affecting millions of people. This is Mystery!

The first questionnaire is designed to help you think about big M Mystery. The second questionnaire asks you to consider the little m mystery of our relationships. And the last questionnaire focuses your attention on "frames" of reference.

MINDFULNESS OF BIG M MYSTERY

Questions about Nature

Spend a moment thinking about what a typical day is like for you. During a typical day, how often do you take time to observe and revel in...

Sunrises...

7	6	5	4	3	2	1
very aware						not at all aware

Sunsets...

7	6	5	4	3	2	1
very aware						not at all aware

Changing cloud formations...

7	6	5	4	3	2	1
very aware				not at all aware		

Storm fronts...

7	6	5	4	3	2	1
very aware				not at all aware		

The sounds and sight of leaves blowing on trees...

7	6	5	4	3	2	1
very aware				not at all aware		

The sound of rain on different surfaces...

7	6	5	4	3	2	1
very aware				not at all aware		

Spiders spinning a web...

7	6	5	4	3	2	1
very aware				not at all aware		

The sound and the feel of wind on your face...

7	6	5	4	3	2	1
very aware				not at all aware		

The night sky...

7   6   5   4   3   2   1

very aware   not at all aware

An ant trail on the sidewalk...

7   6   5   4   3   2   1

very aware   not at all aware

Powerful and destructive natural events...

7   6   5   4   3   2   1

very aware   not at all aware

What makes it easier for you to experience the awe and wonder of nature?

What makes it more difficult?

When you are experiencing the magnificence and power of nature, what differences does it make: in your mind?; in your body?; emotionally?; physically?; relationally?

MINDFULNESS OF LITTLE M MYSTERY OF OUR SOCIAL WORLDS

As you think about your own mindfulness practice, how much time do you spend cultivating mindfulness of your *social worlds*?

When you think of an important relationship that you would like to be better, do you...

Think about what *you* say and do that helps to make the relationship...

7	6	5	4	3	2	1

very aware   not at all aware

Think about what the other person says and does that you don't like and wish were different...

7	6	5	4	3	2	1

very aware   not at all aware

Focus on the issue more than the back and forth conversational flow in which the issue occurs...

7	6	5	4	3	2	1

very aware   not at all aware

Think about interactional patterns that have developed in the relationship over time...

7	6	5	4	3	2	1

very aware   not at all aware

Think about the situations in which the difficult conversations occur...

7	6	5	4	3	2	1

very aware   not at all aware

Think about what you might say or do differently to elicit a better pattern...

7	6	5	4	3	2	1

very aware   not at all aware

Questions About your Relational Habits and Practices

These questions are very broad—they are not relationship or context based. When answering these questions you may want to think specifically about an important relationship or context to help you to more meaningfully answer the question.

When you are in a conversation with _____, how often are you aware of what you're "making" together (i.e., an argument, trust, respect, competition…)?

If a conversation is not going well, how aware are you of your part in making that conversation?

7	6	5	4	3	2	1

very aware   not at all aware

During difficult conversations, how often do you think about the unfolding interactional patterns rather than the content or the ideas?

7	6	5	4	3	2	1

very aware   not at all aware

During a difficult conversation about an important topic, how often are you thinking about what you can say or do *next* to help keep the conversation open?

7	6	5	4	3	2	1

very aware   not at all aware

When beginning a conversation that will be difficult, how much importance do you place on the first few conversational turns?

7	6	5	4	3	2	1

very aware   not at all aware

When beginning a conversation that will be difficult, how aware are you of the way you are speaking and listening?

| 7 | 6 | 5 | 4 | 3 | 2 | 1 |

very aware   not at all aware

Before beginning a conversation that will be difficult and that you've had with this person in the past, how aware are you of the past conversational patterns?

| 7 | 6 | 5 | 4 | 3 | 2 | 1 |

very aware   not at all aware

In situation x (fill in the blank) I tend to do more of (this behavior) _____ as opposed to (other behaviors)
_____

| 7 | 6 | 5 | 4 | 3 | 2 | 1 |

very aware   not at all aware

Think of a person in your life at the moment that you're having difficulty with...

What does s/he say and do that makes it hard for you to stay open and compassionate?

What do you think you say and do that makes it hard for him/her to stay open and compassionate?

What, if anything, are you doing to stay open and curious?

What, if anything, are you doing that reduces your ability to stay open and curious?

Think of this same person and a conversation that is life-giving that the two of you have had...

What is it that you say and do in this conversation that is different than the scenario you just reflected on above?

What does the other person say and do that helps you stay open?

If you could apply one learning from this conversation to help you in your more difficult conversations, what would it be?

QUESTIONS ABOUT FRAMING

I am using the concept of "frame of mind" to refer to what we are paying attention to and how narrow or broad is the focus of our attention.   If we are able to see something in a variety of contexts and recognize that what we are paying attention to is *one of many ways* of seeing the situation, we are creating a broader frame of reference. If what we see or think becomes the totality of the situation then our frame of mind is narrow. Both types of M/mystery include a frame that gets beyond the story and experience of self. However, I think of the frame of Big M Mystery in the context of "powers of 10." It is the willingness and ability to see a situation from enough distance that the situation becomes transformed. For example, in the dream that I described in Chapter 1, when I was no longer "in my skin" but able to see the totality of my life from a perspective of "not me", I immediately shifted to an experience of love and compassion for the many "ME's" throughout my life and for every person in my dream and beyond; the specifics of the situation were transformed from the life of one person to the loving embrace and interconnection of all life forms.

As you answer these questions about framing, think about how large the frame you use typically gets. I realize that frames are "context or situation dependent". However, for purposes of this exercise, explore whether there is a level of framing that seems to be your "default" option.

Generally, how often are you attempting to expand your frame to include the stories of others?

Generally, how often are you attempting to expand your frame to include the experiences of others?

Generally, how often are you attempting to expand your frame to include new ways of thinking about the patterns in particular relationships?

Generally, how often do you expand or contract your frame of reference to focus on time?

Generally, how often are you attempting to expand your frame to include new ways of thinking about problematic episodes?

Generally, how often are you attempting to expand your frame to hold both/and perspectives?

Generally, how often are you attempting to expand your frame to hold paradox (two realities that appear mutually exclusive)?

In general, how often do you consciously attempt to expand your frame of mind?

In what contexts is expanding your frame of mind relatively easy?

In what contexts is it difficult to expand your frame of mind? What are the factors that make it difficult?

Think of a situation in which you made a choice to expand your frame of mind in a difficult situation. What differences did this make for you? What happened as a result of making this choice?

As you think of your own mindfulness practice, how much time do you spend cultivating frames of mind that hold...

Complexity of perspectives and feelings that point in opposite directions...

7	6	5	4	3	2	1
very aware				not at all aware		

Diversity...

7	6	5	4	3	2	1
very aware				not at all aware		

Gratitude...

7	6	5	4	3	2	1
very aware				not at all aware		

The vastness of the universe…

7	6	5	4	3	2	1

very aware   not at all aware

The gift of the moment…

7	6	5	4	3	2	1

very aware   not at all aware

Paradox and confusion…

7	6	5	4	3	2	1

very aware   not at all aware

Uncertainty…

7	6	5	4	3	2	1

very aware   not at all aware

- As you answered the questionnaire, what surprised you?

- What new insights are you gaining?

- How is doing this exercise affecting your stories of your self and of your life?

- How is doing this exercise affecting your stories about your relationships?

- What new actions are you thinking about taking?

- What was most challenging about the exercise?

- How might you think about this exercise in the context of "minding the gap"?

- How might you think about this exercise in the context of M/mystery (the awe and wonder and compassionate embrace about the complexity and diversity of your social world)?

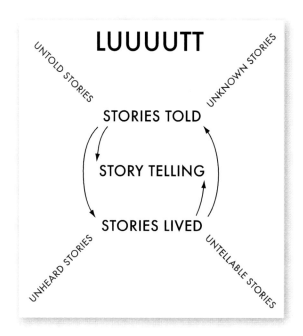

LUUUUTT is an acronym for 1) stories **L**ived; 2) **U**nknown stories, 3) **U**ntold Stories, 4) **U**nheard stories, 5) **U**ntellable stories; 6) Stories **T**old, and 7) story**T**elling. This model is used to explore the gaps between the lived and told stories, stories that are privileged, stories that we choose to tell, stories that are underdeveloped or eerily silent, and the manner of story telling. The model is used to enrich and expand the stories you and others tell by helping us move from slogans and anecdotes to full stories. For example, calling Pop an uncaring and unsupportive Father is a slogan and not a full story. To the extent that I am telling fuller stories of who Pop is, I am able to live with complexity and greater compassion. This model also draws attention to the *way* that we tell our stories and its effects on others.

INSTRUCTIONS:

1. You have stories about yourself that are guiding how you think of yourself and how you act. Spend about 1 hour writing a letter to your self. In the letter, describe your self as if you are introducing yourself to the You who is curious to know as much as possible about you.

2. Begin with the Daisy model. Put yourself in the center of the daisy and use each petal to identify a different aspect of the person called "You." For example, my daisy would include mother, daughter, grandmother, retired professor, widow, visionary, friend, colleague, woman in transition...

3. Begin with the stories told: these are the stories that you tell about yourself and that others would recognize as a description of you. Walk through the daisy and describe the stories told of each of the petals

4. Now write about the untold stories: thinking about each petal on the daisy, what stories about yourself have you chosen to keep to yourself. What differences would it make it you made these stories known?

5. Now write about the untellable stories: The stories that have been too painful to tell but that you are ready to write about. Hold yourself with compassion as you tell these stories.

6. Now reflect on the unheard stories: stories that others have been trying to tell you that you have been unable or unwilling to hear. What stories about you would they include in this letter? Write about these things.

7. Now reflect on the manner of storytelling. What is the tone in your letter as you write about yourself? Are you holding the various aspects of yourself with compassion and love? Are there aspects of your stories that are difficult for you to hold compassionately? Explore ways in which you can enlarge your lens to hold greater complexity.

8. Lastly, are there new stories about You that you want to tell and cultivate? Are there missing petals on the daisy? What are they? How do you imagine your life being different if you told and lived into these new stories.?

INDIVIDUAL OR GROUP REFLECTIONS AFTER THE EXERCISE:

- As you were writing the stories of you, what surprised you?

- What new insights are you gaining about the power of your stories in shaping how you see yourself; how you act; what you don't see?

- What was most challenging about the exercise?

- How might you think about this exercise in the context of "minding the gap"?

- How might you think about this exercise in the context of mystery (the awe and wonder and compassionate embrace about the complexity and diversity of your social world)?

EXERCISE #4: GRATITUDE AND MOMENTS OF GRACE

TIME ALLOTMENT: 1 DAY

We live in a world filled with many things including beauty, wonder, kindness, love, laughter, joy, moments of grace... Most of us don't pay enough attention to these aspects of our lives and, consequently, we miss the opportunity for experiencing abundant gratitude and grace.

Spend a day looking for the various aspects of our worlds that invite you to experience gratitude and moments of grace. The moment that you become aware that you are feeling stressed, or angry, or annoyed, own it, acknowledge it, recognize it has something to say to you and then seek out a moment of grace and something about which to be grateful. Experience what shifting your attention to this aspect of your world does to your mind, your heart, and your frame of reference.

INDIVIDUAL OR GROUP REFLECTIONS AFTER THE EXERCISE:

- As you spent the day focusing on gratitude and moments of grace, what surprised you?

- What new insights are you gaining about the power of framing in terms of what you see and don't see?

- What was most challenging about the exercise?

- How might you think about this exercise in the context of "minding the gap"?

- How might you think about this exercise in the context of mystery (the awe and wonder and compassionate embrace about the complexity and diversity of your social world)?

TIME ALLOTMENT: 30 MINUTES

Ask someone whom you know and trust to reflect on the ways that you help him/her stay open, curious, compassionate and engaged in your conversations. Discuss the things you say and do that make it more difficult to stay open, curious, compassionate and engaged. Explore when these different ways of being together happen? What specifically do you say and do that helps your partner?

INDIVIDUAL OR GROUP REFLECTIONS AFTER THE EXERCISE:

- What surprised you about this conversation?

- What new insights about yourself are you seeing as a result of this conversation?

- What are your takeaways?—What new practices might you want to engage in as a result of this conversation?

Our stories about ourselves are embedded in our relationships with others and in our experiences. Often times the stories others have about us become our stories and we become authored by them instead of authoring or at least co-authoring the stories. This exercise is designed to provide a way for you to work with the aspects of your self that you are having a difficult time embracing and exploring where those stories about you are coming from and how much you want to privilege them.

INSTRUCTIONS:

1. Make a list of the aspects of you that you are having difficulty loving and embracing. For example, "I'm too impatient"; "I'm too judgmental"…

2. For each of these parts of you that are difficult to love, put the aspect at the center of the Daisy Model. For example,

if you are struggling with two aspects of yourself, each of these would become a separate Daisy with one aspect at the center. You would have 2 Daisies in all. Using the above example, the center of one daisy would say "I'm too impatient" and the center of the second daisy would say, "I'm too judgmental".

3. Think of the people and circumstances that reinforce this aspect of you that you find difficult to love and embrace. Each person or circumstance would be a petal on the Daisy. For example, for the "I'm too impatient" daisy, the petals might include the people in your life who have criticized you for your impatience. Or think of circumstances where patience just doesn't seem possible and you feel bad about it. For example, perhaps you find that you have a very difficult time with slow drivers on the highway and it gets your blood boiling. Or you find yourself yelling at your kids in the morning because they are going to be late, yet again, for school.

4. Now spend time with each petal. What do you hear each petal saying to do? What do you want them to know about their effect on you? Explore the full range of your emotions as you speak with each petal and embrace these emotions as having something important to say. Name the kind of relationship you want to have with each of these petals.

5. Which petals have the strongest voice? What has enabled their voice to be so strong and powerful?

6. Observe which petals are missing that would change the story you have about this difficult aspect of yourself. What differences would it make if these petals were present?

7. If you didn't add M/mystery as a petal, do so now. What differences does it make if you think of this aspect of yourself that is hard to love with a petal of Mystery as the strongest voice? Use the powers of 10 exercise to experiment with this aspect of you and Mystery? Zoom out by a few powers of 10 so the daisy is floating somewhere in a cosmos filled with awe and wonder. What differences does it make if you make mystery the loudest petal on your Daisy (recognizing and holding the complexity of your self with compassion and love).

8. If there was one thing you could change at this moment to help you love and embrace these more difficult aspects of you, what would it be?

9. Now make a commitment to do it everyday and see what happens.

INDIVIDUAL OR GROUP REFLECTIONS AFTER THE EXERCISE:

- As you reflect on the Daisies that you have made, what surprises you?

- What new insights are you gaining about the power of framing in terms of what you see and don't see?

- What was most challenging about the exercise?

- How might you think about this exercise in the context of "minding the gap"?

- How might you think about this exercise in the context of M/mystery (the powers of 10 and/or the awe and wonder and compassionate embrace about the complexity and diversity of your social world)?

7

Mindfulness of Making & Managing Meaning

The Second Set of Practices: Mindfulness of Making and Managing Meaning Through the Stories we Tell

Among other things, practicing mindfulness of making and managing meaning involves remembering that:

- Stories grow out of our experiences and we are shaped by them

- All stories are local, incomplete and unfinished

- Curiosity deepens appreciation for the complexity of stories

- Deep listening fosters the exploration of the fuller story

- The manner of storytelling affects the willingness of others to stay open and curious

- Practice M/mystery as a lens for developing greater compassion for the stories of others that are antithetical to your stories

Before you begin this next set of practices, I'd like you to take time to reflect on each of the bulleted points. Are you finding that these phrases are common sense? It's difficult to dispute the wisdom of them, isn't it?   My experience however is that this list is easier said than done, especially in the moment when someone is saying or doing something that is "pushing my buttons." Consequently, the set of exercises in this section are meant to help you translate these ideas into ways of seeing and acting throughout the day.

I also invite you to reflect for a moment on the power of stories in shaping *every* aspect of our lives. We are guided by the stories we tell, which affect what we see and how we experience the world, which guide the stories we tell, and so on.

I have a story that the phrase "seeing is believing" should really be reversed: believing is seeing. We tell stories to tame the terrors of life, to help us know how to act in this situation as opposed to that one, to help us cope with why bad things happen to good people, and so on. The stories we tell, especially the highest-level stories that guide what we see and how we act, become the lens for what we see. If we don't have a story for a situation, it can be quite unsettling. And psychologists tell us that if a person cannot construct a viable narrative for one's life, it can precipitate deep depression, insanity, or suicide. The stories we tell matter!

My husband Barnett has been my profound teacher in the power of our stories in ennobling us to act beyond what we thought was possible. When Barnett was diagnosed with cancer he made an important declaration that guided the last two years of his life. He said, "It has taken me 65 years to be the person that I am today and I'm not going to let cancer define my last years." The *doing* of this declaration included privileging the story of Mystery and moments of grace. And because these stories were the ones that were consistently the highest context for Barnett, he was able to see and experience beauty, acts of kindness, joy and laughter, and profound love even when he was in tremendous pain and his body was failing him. Believing is seeing!!

The exercises that are included in this section will expand on each of the bulleted points above. But before we move to the first exercise, I want to bring in another voice that has much to teach us. Bud Goodall is a friend and colleague of Barnett's and mine. Bud died on Saturday from pancreatic cancer at the age of 59. When he learned 14 months ago that he had Stage 4 pancreatic cancer he knew his time was limited. Among others, he leaves behind a wife, a son, and many students, scholars and colleagues who have benefited from his life and his words. One month before he died, he said this in his blog (http://www.hlgoodall.com/Blog/):

> Let's use this timeless energy for immortality to make out of the everyday a richer more poetic narrative - a narrative about who we are as creative spiritual beings; about us as women and men on a noble quest for meanings, for justice, for a way of being in this world that prepares us best for whatever comes next; and then let's devote part of each day to figuring out what we must do to achieve our starry night destiny, our own personal narrative's most satisfying end.

To this end, let us begin the practices to ennoble us to achieve our starry night destiny of greater compassion and love.

EXERCISE #1: USING THE HIERARCHY MODEL

TIME ALLOTMENT: 1 WEEK

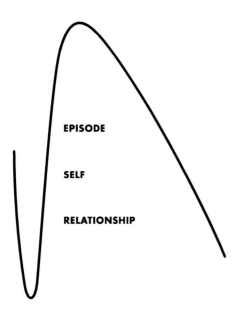

EPISODE

SELF

RELATIONSHIP

The Hierarchy Model is designed to help you understand the highest contexts and stories you have about any given situation that guide what you see and how you act. Every event includes several types of stories we are telling; for example, the actual situation or the episode, one's sense of self, the importance of the relationship, the cultural stories and cultural constraints, etc. But not every story has equal weight. Exploring and naming your higher level contexts can be extremely helpful in understanding the different frames and forces that are contributing to your stories and the unfolding interactional pattern.

In the diagram above, the person is privileging the episode, or the situation, followed by the story of self and then the relationship. The person in this illustration is Philip's brother on the tennis court. Remember I mentioned him when I introduced the use of the hierarchy model a few chapters ago. Philip's brother loves to play and he enjoys the thrills of winning, so his highest context is the game of tennis while they are on the court. He is also good, so his story of self as a good and competitive player is just below the importance of the game itself. His relationship with Philip is the least important during the game. Philip's relationship with his brother is more important to him than the game itself. So Philip's highest-level context is relationship. Naming this as the highest context has helped Philip understand why he lets up if he's beating his brother on the court and why his brother is unrelenting in his desire to win.

The hierarchy model helps us name what's most important in any given situation and to remember that our stories and our highest level of context will influence what we see, what we don't see, and how we act. The broader the contextual frame, the more possibilities there are for holding complexity and paradox.

For example, a natural response for me after Barnett's death would have been to keep "self" at the highest level of context. Doing so would have created a space for the issues and fears that I have: my heart is broken; life will never be the same; I'm alone now; who will take care of me if something happens to me?; why did this happen to me?; I can't imagine ever getting over this loss... All of these statements are "true" so it isn't as if these are exaggerated stories. However, can you feel in your body how "self" as the highest level of context creates a tight and constraining frame? There are many other "truths" to the situation of being a widow that won't get a hearing if I keep privileging self as the highest context. I am not saying to avoid the stories and perspectives in which "self" is the highest context. What I am suggesting is that we cultivate mindfulness of our higher-level contexts and we remember that "what we pay attention to grows."

Part of my daily practice has been to keep both types of M/ mystery as the highest-level story. I'm deliberately expanding my frame to include moments of grace, complexity, and paradox as a normalizing lens for viewing what's in front of me. Because of that deliberate choice, I am seeing the wonders of nature, the daily acts of kindness that are everywhere, and even paranormal experiences that lead to me believe that Barnett has just paid me a visit. Notice how this level of context creates a much larger space for unexpected things to show up in ways that I can see and celebrate.

INSTRUCTIONS:

1. Think of a relational issue in which your highest level story has been "self" and you have found that, even though the stories are true, they have not been useful for expanding your heart and mind and cultivating a more compassionate relationship. Now do the following:

2. Put either type of M/mystery as the highest level of context. If the situation involves another person, putting mystery as the highest level will make a space for you to include awe and wonder about the complexity of you, the other person, and of your relationship. For example, take time to explore and to name the aspects of you, the person and the situation that are much more complex than you have allowed for. This complexity includes the whole range of possibilities—emotions, stories that you're unaware of, experiences of long ago that still cast its shadow, internal voices that affect what your partner sees (or doesn't see) and how she feels about herself... Allow complexity and the unknown to be your lens instead of "self" and see where that takes you. What openings does this lens allow that the lens of self didn't?

3. If you want to experiment with an even broader lens, play with Mystery as the highest level of context. Imagine the situation using the lens of "powers of 10". There will become a point at which the issue is not longer relevant— the frame has transformed it into something else. The paradox of Mystery as the highest level is that it will hold paradox—in one sense the issue may be crucially important and in another sense the issue is not important at all. As you are experimenting with Mystery, notice what thoughts, feelings, and bodily sensations emerge and how they change.

Once you have imagined M/mystery as the highest level of context, spend time every day nurturing that frame. When you start seeing yourself getting back into "self" as the higher-level context, acknowledge the truth to those stories and then gently shift to M/mystery as the higher level context. Repeat as often as you need to.

Do this exercise for 1 week and observe the differences from day 1 to day 7.

- As you deliberately worked with enlarging your frame, what surprised you?

- What new insights are you gaining?

- How is doing this exercise affecting your stories of the situation and the people involved?

- What new actions are you thinking about taking or have you already taken?

- What was most challenging about the exercise?

- How might you think about this exercise in the context of "minding the gap"?

- How might you think about this exercise in the context of mystery as a normalizing lens (the awe and wonder and compassionate embrace about the complexity and diversity of your social world)?

LUUUUTT is an acronym for 1) stories <u>L</u>ived; 2) <u>U</u>nknown stories, 3) <u>U</u>ntold Stories, 4) <u>U</u>nheard stories, 5) <u>U</u>ntellable stories; 6) Stories <u>T</u>old, and 7) story<u>T</u>elling. This model is used to explore the gaps between the lived and told stories, stories that are privileged, stories that are underdeveloped or eerily silent, and the manner of story telling. The model is used to enrich and expand the stories you and others tell by helping us move from slogans and anecdotes to full stories. To the extent that we are telling fuller stories, we are able to live with complexity and greater compassion. We also become more mindful of the way that we tell our stories and its effects on others.

INSTRUCTIONS:

Think of a situation involving others that you are struggling with. Spend time reflecting and perhaps even writing about the following:

*   Begin with the stories told: these are the stories that you and others tell about the situation and/or the person. As

you reflect on the stories told, notice whether they are full and complex stories or whether the told story has become a slogan or anecdote.

- Now think about the untold stories: the stories about the situation/person that you have chosen to keep to yourself. If you were to make these stories known, whom would you be most likely to tell? Whom would you be least likely to tell? What differences would it make it you made these stories known and to whom would it make a difference? What differences is it making that you are not telling these stories?

- Now turn your attention to the untellable stories: The stories that have been too painful or risky to tell. What differences do you notice between the "untold" and the "untellable" stories. If you were to tell these stories, whom would you be most likely to tell? Whom would you be least likely to tell? What differences would it make it you made these stories known? To whom would it make the biggest difference? What differences is it making that you are *not* telling these stories?

- Reflect on the unheard stories: stories that others have been trying to tell you that you have been unable or unwilling to hear. What stories about the situation/person do you think they would tell? What stories about you do you think they would tell?

- Now think about the manner of storytelling. When you think of the ways you and others have talked about the situation/person, how would you characterize the manner of storytelling? Is there a tone of certainty or stridency that keeps cropping up? How about body postures? What connections do you see between the manner of talking about the situation/person and the difficulty you and others are experiencing? What differences would it make if the manner of storytelling were different? What changes do you think would make the most difference?

- Lastly, are there new stories about the situation that you want to tell and cultivate? What are they? How do you imagine the situation being different if you told and lived into these new stories.? What will you need to do to cultivate these richer stories?

INDIVIDUAL & GROUP REFLECTIONS AFTER THE EXERCISE:

- What surprised you as you were doing this exercise?

- What new insights are you gaining about the power of stories in shaping how we see ourselves; how we act; what we don't see?

- What was most challenging about the exercise?

- How might you think about this exercise in the context of "minding the gap"?

- How might you think about this exercise in the context of mystery (the awe and wonder and compassionate embrace about the complexity and diversity of your social world)?

This exercise is designed to enrich the stories you have about a person or group whom you have tended to describe in "slogans" or "antidotes". It is also an exercise in mystery: of storying the person or group in more complex and compassionate ways.

INSTRUCTIONS:

Take a sheet of paper and write the name of the person or group whom you would like to explore in the center of the daisy. It can be as specific as "my bitchy cousin Ida" or as general (if you find yourself stereotyping) as "right wing conservatives" or "lefty, liberal democrats".

1. Begin by naming the various stories you have about this person or group by putting a headline for each story on a separate petal. For example, for either of the above

groups, petals might include, "scary; mean spirited; socialist; unpatriotic; naïve; ignorant…"

2. Look over the petals. What strikes you about what you have written? Is there a theme to the petals that you hadn't realized?

3. Now add petals that are not your story, but the story of others more sympathetic to the person or group?

4. Look over those petals. Is there a theme to the petals that you hadn't realized? What differences do you notice between your stories and theirs?

5. Think of the circumstances that have shaped the person or group to act in the ways that they do. Does thinking about the person or group within a larger system shift your own thinking about the person or group?

6. Now add petals that have no content. Imagine these petals as aspects of the person or group that you don't know but are nonetheless shaping them.

7. Observe which petals are missing that would change the story you have about the person or group. What differences would it make if these petals were present? Now imagine the possibility of the empty petals or the petals that you have storied affecting the missing petals that you wish were present.

8. If you didn't add Mystery as a petal, do so now. What differences does it make if you think of the person or group through a petal of Mystery (use the powers of 10 exercise to experiment with this aspect of you, the person or group and Mystery)? What differences does it make if you make mystery the loudest petal on this Daisy (recognizing and acknowledging the complexity of the person or group).

INDIVIDUAL & GROUP REFLECTIONS AFTER THE EXERCISE:

- As you did this exercise, what surprised you?

- What new insights are you gaining?

- How is this exercise affecting your stories about the difficult person or group?

- What stories might you include to increase the complexity of the person or group?

- What was most challenging about the exercise?

- How might you think about this exercise in the context of "minding the gap"?

- How might you think about this exercise in the context of mystery (the awe and wonder and compassionate embrace about the complexity and diversity of your social world)?

EXERCISE #4: DEEP LISTENING EXERCISE

TIME ALLOTMENT: 30 MINUTES

Think of a person with ideas or perspectives that you have a difficult time taking seriously but that are important to the person. Spend time with this person, the purpose of which is to more deeply enter their world to see the issue as they do. Ask genuine questions out of curiosity that will enrich your understanding of the person and the issue. Your goal is not to change your mind or theirs, but to enrich your own stories and experiences of the person through curiosity and deep listening.

For example, my mom loves to shop and my step-dad just doesn't understand that. This would be a great exercise for Pop as a way to enter my mom's world to understand what shopping means to her and why she enjoys it so much.

INDIVIDUAL & GROUP REFLECTIONS AFTER THE EXERCISE:

- As you did this exercise, what surprised you?

- What new insights are you gaining about curiosity and listening?

- How has this exercise changed your stories about the person and/or the issue s/he endorses? How has this exercise changed your stories of yourself?

- What stories changed about the person and/or the issue as a result of curiosity and deep listening?

- What was most challenging about the exercise?

- How might you think about this exercise in the context of "minding the gap"?

- How might you think about this exercise in the context of mystery (the awe and wonder and compassionate embrace about the complexity and diversity of your social world)?

EXERCISE #5: USING VARIOUS CMM MODELS TO ENRICH STORIES OF THOSE NOT LIKE YOU

TIME ALLOTMENT: 1 HOUR

This exercise is designed to explore ways of enriching stories of people not like you.

INSTRUCTIONS:

1. Choose someone who is different from you in belief, ideology, background, or culture. Look closely. Note insignia; styles of dress, hair, posture, etc.

2. Begin with curiosity, something like "what kind of person is this that is much more complex than I could know?" Work within a context that this person was born into a social system not of her choosing; that she is partly, but only partly, responsible for the patterns of communication that has made her what she is; and that, within her own social world, she is doing the best she can and doing what she thinks is right and/or what she ought or has to do.

3. Then use CMM's heuristics as a discipline to build a set of stories about this person.

4. Use the daisy model to see this person at the center of multiple conversations that have contributed to the person she is today in all of her complexity.

5. Use the concept of logical force or sense of oughtness to infer what she believes that she should/should not do.

6. Use the LUUUUTT model to explore possible unknown, untellable, unheard, and untold stories; the tension between stories lived and stories told; the manner of storytelling.

7. And when you've done all this, focus on your own state of compassionate storytelling as a function of being mindful of a social world not like yours.

INDIVIDUAL & GROUP REFLECTIONS AFTER THE EXERCISE:

- As you did this exercise, what surprised you?

- What new insights are you gaining?

- How is this exercise affecting your stories about someone not like you?

- What stories did you include to increase the complexity of the person or group?

- What was most challenging about the exercise?

- How might you think about this exercise in the context of "minding the gap"?

- How might you think about this exercise in the context of mystery (the awe and wonder and compassionate embrace about the complexity and diversity of your social world)?

EXERCISE #6: PERSPECTIVE TAKING

TIME ALLOTMENT: 1 HOUR

This exercise requires you to tell 3 very different stories about the same experience. It's designed to help you recognize that all stories are partial and incomplete and the story you choose to tell foregrounds some things while making other things opaque.

INSTRUCTIONS:

1. Choose a situation that you find difficult and you have had a clear-cut story about. For example, perhaps you are raising a difficult child and your story is that she is selfish and self-centered. Write the specifics of this story being as detailed as possible.

2. Using the same situation, tell a second very different but plausible story. Make the details of this second story as elaborate and detailed as possible. For example, I have a child that feels safe enough with me to push the boundaries and rules of our home...

3. Using the same situation, tell a third very different but plausible story. Make the details of this third story as elaborate and detailed as possible. For example, I have a child that is acting age appropriate as she discovers who she is...

4. Spend time with each other these stories and reflect on the following:

   a. Why have I chosen to foreground the first story?

   b. What differences would it make if I foregrounded the other stories?

   c. When I think about each of these stories separately, what differences does it make in my body and my emotions and mind if I'm privileging any one of these stories?

   d. What new meanings emerge as a result of creating three different plausible stories about the situation?

e. Remembering that the question isn't which story is more accurate but which story helps you make the best relationship possible, which of these stories (or perhaps a new story not yet spoken) will help make the most desirable social world? What differences do you think acting into this story makes?

INDIVIDUAL & GROUP REFLECTIONS AFTER THE EXERCISE:

- As you did this exercise, what surprised you?

- What new insights are you gaining?

- How is this exercise affecting the ways you're thinking about stories?

- What stories did you include to increase the complexity of the person or group?

- What was most challenging about the exercise?

- How might you think about this exercise in the context of "minding the gap"?

- How might you think about this exercise in the context of mystery (the awe and wonder and compassionate embrace about the complexity and diversity of your social world)?

8

Mindfulness of Coordinating Actions

The Third Set of Practices: Mindfulness of coordinating our actions; or said differently, mindfulness of the ways a conversation unfolds over time.

These mindfulness practices invite you to remember that:

- All conversations have multiple turns (you say something, I respond to what you've said, you respond to what I've said…and if the relationship is an established one we will bring in "the history of what we've said and done…").

- Each turn is a response to something and it elicits a response.

- Every turn opens up or closes down possibilities.

- The quality of our conversations affect selves, relationships, and our social worlds.

- We get what we make.

- Practice M/mystery as a lens for developing compassion and awe and wonder for the complexity of the coordinated dances we engage in moment by moment.

I want to begin this section with a true story about two men ages 41 and 48. One of these men is a software engineer. Both have Facebook pages; these are the stories they each tell on their Facebook pages about the importance of life. Mr. Holbrook: "Enjoy every day to its fullest because we only get one pass at life"; and, Mr. Ziesmer: "I'm an easy going man, who doesn't sweat the "dumb" or "stupid" things that happen in everyday life. Life is way too short for stupid. I hate to have to argue about or to even address these issues".

In March 2011 these men, who didn't know each other, were driving on Old First Street in Livermore, California. Something happened and they got into a traffic related dispute. Holbrooke produced a knife and stabbed Ziesmer. Ziesmer drove himself to a hospital but was later pronounced dead. Holbrook received facial abrasions in the fight. He was jailed without bail and he is being tried from murder.

I tell this story to make an important point about our social worlds: the stories we tell never clearly translate into the lives that we live. And sometimes our actions are antithetical to what we believe and they lead to unintended and tragic consequences. One way of understanding the contradictions between lived and told stories is that our stories are *lived in the coordinated dance with others*. And people say and do things that "push our buttons!"...and when our buttons are pushed we often feel compelled to act in a particular way. CMM calls this "logical force." It's the idea that our interactions create an energy field that we sometimes get sucked into. The energy compels us to say and do things that we know isn't in our or the other's, or the relationship's best interest. You have a fight with a loved one, for example, and walk away scratching your head saying, how did that happen?

One of the most important set of practices to grow your ability to act with greater awareness are those that focus on ways that you coordinate with others. This requires that you think of your communicating as a sequence of actions that, over time, create patterns, and these patterns are always creating our social worlds.

The practices in this chapter will focus on your ability to be mindful of turn-by-turn interactions, of how these interactions affect how compelled you feel to act in particular and unintended ways, and to look for places in a conversation where what you say and do next will make an important difference in the trajectory of the conversation.

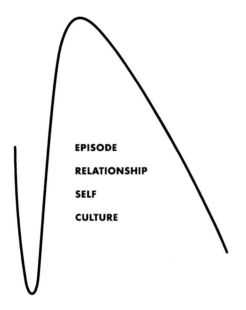

EPISODE

RELATIONSHIP

SELF

CULTURE

The Hierarchy Model is designed to help you understand the highest contexts and stories you have about any given situation that guide what you see and how you act. Every event includes several types of stories we are telling; for example, the actual situation or the episode, one's sense of self, the importance of the relationship, the cultural stories and cultural constraints, etc. But not every story has equal weight. Exploring and naming your higher level contexts can be extremely helpful in understanding the different frames and forces that are contributing to your stories *and the unfolding interactional pattern.*

INSTRUCTIONS:

1. Think of a situation in which you and someone you know have an on-going and repetitive pattern that you would like to change. For example, perhaps you and your roommate have the same conflict over who will clean the house and how clean the house will be.

2. Once you have identified the situation, think about the highest-level story you have that you think is guiding your actions. For example, perhaps your highest-level story is that your roommate is a slob, it's driving you nuts, and you don't want to continually be picking up after her. This story compels you, especially when you come home to a living room with her stuff strewn around it, to tell her to pick up her junk and keep the common areas of the house clean. Which in turn, makes a fight between the two of you.

3. In this situation you have identified the highest stories as that of "self" and "culture" (in your family of origin, people are respectful about how common areas are treated in a house).

4. Now that you have identified the highest-level stories, spend time exploring the ways in which these stories are compelling you to act as you have.

5. Shift your awareness to a very different higher-level story of relationship, other, or mystery. As your awareness shifts to these other possible higher-level stories, imagine how you might act differently into the situation if your actions were based on these higher-level stories. For example, if you make *the relationship* with your roommate the highest level of context for your actions, what might you say or do differently when you walk into your home and find your roommate's things strewn around the common living areas? If you make *other* the highest context, this will focus your attention on her story and needs. In this case, it will sensitize you to your roommate's 60-hour work week due to staff shortages.

6. Using a broader frame for thinking about the situation, think specifically about what you would say first when you walk into the house. Anticipate how you can respond differently if your roommate says the same things that have elicited frustration from you. The goal of this portion of the exercise is for you to imagine what specifically you can say and do that supports the relationship, other, or mystery as your highest-level context.

7. Once you have imagined new ways of responding, try them out the next time you are confronted with the situation.

Observe the differences in your partner's responses. Did you help evoke or elicit a more desirable and helpful response from your partner? Observe the ways in which you are responding to your partner. Are you able to hold the situation more compassionately?

8. Repeat this exercise as needed in situations with other people.

INDIVIDUAL & GROUP REFLECTIONS AFTER THE EXERCISE:

- As you did this exercise, what surprised you?

- What new insights are you gaining?

- How is this exercise affecting your mindfulness of higher-level stories and your actions?

- How did putting the relationship, other, or mystery as the highest level of context change the way you thought about the person or situation?

- What was most challenging about the exercise?

- How might you think about this exercise in the context of "minding the gap"?

- How might you think about this exercise in the context of mystery (the awe and wonder and compassionate embrace about the complexity and diversity of your social world)?

EXERCISE #2: USING THE SERPENTINE MODEL TO IDENTIFY CONVERSATIONAL TURNS

TIME ALLOTMENT: 1 HOUR

The Serpentine Model is a way of describing a sequence of actions through time and the ways that each act elicits a particular response from the participants. This model can also be used in conjunction with the Hierarchy Model to help identify the highest levels of context and/or to identify forces, or the sense of oughtness, that participants often experience. Each box represents a "turn" in the conversation (what each person says and does). If both participants in a conversation are interested in exploring their frustrating interaction, they can use the Serpentine Model to recount each turn and illuminate the various levels of context. A person can also individually use the model as a way of exploring a difficult, confusing, or frustrating conversation that is occurring in the moment, that has occurred in the past, or that is a repetitive pattern occurring over time.

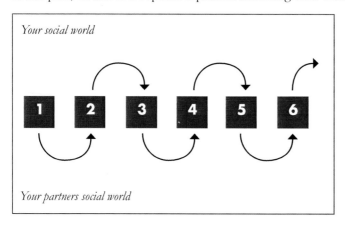

INSTRUCTIONS:

Think of a situation in which you and someone you know are having an on-going and repetitive pattern that you would like to change.

Diagram each turn using the serpentine model. Think of the diagram as a "script" that you are writing: He says this (specify what he says/does and how he says it); I respond with this (specify what you say/do and how you say it); he responds in this way; I respond to him by saying/doing this, and so on.

Script out the entire turn by turn interaction from beginning to end.

Once you've done that, spend time feeling in your body the ways that your interactions are compelling each of you to act in particular ways. This means putting yourself in your partner's position as well as your own.

If you feel comfortable enough, talk with your partner about this exercise and your observations about the interactional pattern.

EXERCISE #3: BUILDING ON THE LAST EXERCISE BY IDENTIFYING CRITICAL MOMENTS OR BIFURCATION POINTS FOR CHANGE

TIME ALLOTMENT: 1 HOUR

CMM has developed a concept called "bifurcation points." If you think of a fork in the road you know that your subsequent experience will be quite different depending on which road you choose to take. An unfolding conversation is like this as well. What you or another person say or do "next" can be quite significant in terms of how the rest of the conversation goes. Part of mindfulness practice involves being sensitive to the "next turn" or the next thing you say or do that can help or hurt the unfolding interaction.

INSTRUCTIONS:

1. Go back to the turn-by-turn diagram that you have done in Exercise #2.

2. Focus on the conversational turns that you took. As you think about each of your turns, imagine what you could have said or done differently to help create a more satisfying conversational outcome between you and your partner.

3. Now play out the conversation in your imagination feeling in your body the differences that these new turns might make for you and your partner. Imagine as concretely as possible the differences that your partner will experience as a result of these new turns.

4. End this exercise by talking with your partner about what you have discovered about your own part in the pattern that you both don't like and your commitment to helping

to change the pattern by responding differently in the future.

5. If you're not comfortable talking with your partner, practice these changes the next time you have a conversation and observe the differences.

INDIVIDUAL & GROUP REFLECTIONS AFTER THE EXERCISE:

- What surprised you as you were doing both of these exercises?

- What new insights are you gaining about the power of our joint actions in making a frustrating or satisfying conversation?...in making a frustrating or satisfying relationship?...in helping you think about your own "agency" and ability to act differently?

- Are you thinking differently about the sense of "oughtness to respond" you feel based on what someone has just said or done? What differences do your think it will make for you to become more mindful of this?

- Are you thinking differently about critical moments in a conversation knowing that what you say or do next will affect your partner, the unfolding interaction, and the relationship? What differences do you think it will make for you to become more mindful of this?

- What was most challenging about the exercise?

- How might you think about this exercise in the context of "minding the gap"?

- How might you think about this exercise in the context of mystery (the awe and wonder and compassionate embrace about the complexity and diversity of our social worlds)?

EXERCISE #4: RELATIONSHIP WATCHING

TIME ALLOTMENT: 1 WEEK

Spend a week watching and looking for examples of people engaged in communication patterns that help make openness, compassion, and trust (you can even do this in fictional settings such as literature, television, theatre, etc.). Observe what they say and do in the back and forth flow of their communication. Keep a journal of what you observe, diagramming the conversational turns if you can. At the end of the week look over your journal and reflect on any patterns or themes in the things people said and did with one another. For example, when do you notice shifts in tone and content? What were people saying and doing that shifted the tone? How are people navigating their differences? Did you notice moments in which what someone said or did made a clear difference in what happened next?

INDIVIDUAL & GROUP REFLECTIONS AFTER THE EXERCISE:

- What surprised you as you were doing this exercise?

- What new insights are you gaining about the power of our joint actions in making a satisfying conversation?…in making a satisfying relationship?

- What skills and abilities did you observe?

- What is the most important take-away for you as you observed examples of good interactions?

- What was most challenging about the exercise?

- How might you think about this exercise in the context of "minding the gap"?

- How might you think about this exercise in the context of mystery (the awe and wonder and compassionate embrace about the complexity and diversity of our social worlds)?

TIME ALLOTMENT: 1 WEEK

Spend the next week being aware of the times that you are involved in any type of difficult conversation. While you are in the situation, think about the power of the next turn. Focus on what you can say or do next that will help everyone involved stay more open and compassionate. Now, act into the turn and see what happens. Keep a journal throughout the week to use as a springboard for your own reflections about the differences your "next turn" made for all of the participants involved.

INDIVIDUAL & GROUP REFLECTIONS AFTER DOING BOTH EXERCISES:

- What surprised you as you were doing this exercise?

- What new insights are you gaining about the power of your next turn in making a satisfying conversation?…in making a satisfying relationship?

- What skills and abilities did you use? Did the use of any of these tools surprise you?

- What is the most important take-away for you as a result of doing this exercise?

- What was most challenging about the exercise?

- How might you think about this exercise in the context of "minding the gap"?

- How might you think about this exercise in the context of mystery (the awe and wonder and compassionate embrace about the complexity and diversity of our social worlds)?

9

Mindfulness of Making Better Social Worlds

The Fourth Set Of Practices: Mindfulness Of Making Better Social Worlds.

These mindfulness practices invite you to remember to:

- Think in terms of patterns and relationships

- Recognize your part in making the patterns of which you are a part

- Develop habits and skills that foster mindfulness of various perspectives

- Develop habits and skills that foster curiosity and compassion

- Practice M/mystery as a lens for developing compassion, humility, and awe and wonder for the complexity of our social worlds

We have come to the last set of practices and, in some respects, the most controversial. Over the years, Barnett and I have written about and stated publicly our commitment to making *better social worlds*. And of course this always begs the questions, "better by whose standards? Isn't this just a way of privileging your own world view of what better means and looks like in practice?" Barnett's response has always been to say that we don't know what better looks like until we co-construct it together. But if we focus on the *pattern* of communication, the best possible outcomes will happen.

Although I agree with Barnett's answers to these questions, my response is a bit different. I would add to his comments by saying that anything we can do to grow our ability to hold complexity and our differences, to stay open and curious to the lives, experiences, and world-views of others, and to grow our hearts to hold and enact compassion and love will make better social worlds. The bulleted points above help us to do these things as do all of the practices in the last three chapters.

This chapter "puts it all together." I offer no additional practices in this section. What I am offering is a personal story of my attempt to make a better social world in a very difficult situation using the practices in this book.

A DIFFICULT FAMILY SITUATION

I recently learned of a situation involving a family member that, if not taken care of, will have significant legal and financial implications. When I talked with the person about taking care of it, his response was indefatigable protestations of unfairness and consequently he didn't want to do anything about it.

Pause. This is a fork in the road for me, or what CMM calls a bifurcation point. The easy thing for me to do is to walk away from it, especially since this is what the family member wanted to do. But his response really angered me and I knew that if I walked away from it my anger would seethe, my relationship with him would suffer, and the situation would eventually affect other people in his and my life. I didn't want any of these things to happen, so I knew that I needed to continue engaging this issue with the person.

This was not an easy thing to do because this person doesn't like to "stay present" in emotionally difficult situations. His learned response over the years is to physically get up and walk away or, if he does stay in the room, to tune out the conversation and act as if the situation does not exist. In my first few attempts to talk with him he did both of these things. My story for his behavior is "willful ignorance" and my inner response was anger and disgust.

Pause. This is another fork in the road. There are now two responses that would be easy for me. The first would be to walk away from it, especially since I have tried to have follow-up conversations. The second would be to lash out in anger and disgust at what I perceive to be his selfishness and lack of regard for his family.

I also realized that these situations are the critical moments in which what I say and do next will cast a long shadow. Before going back to the person to talk again about the situation, I spent time clarifying my highest-level stories (or what CMM calls highest level contexts) and what kind of social world I wanted to make in this situation and in the relationship. What I wanted to make was a resolution that honored the legal and ethical obligations this person had legally agreed to. I also wanted to make a relationship that would help me move through my anger and disgust. And I wanted to make a situation in which the other people affected by this legal situation came away with stronger ties toward each other. Another way of saying this is that I wanted to make a *better* social world.

I made a conscious choice to put mystery as the highest-level context for the conversations we would have. The practice of this for me involves simultaneously holding him and his needs, me and my needs, and the unfolding conversation that we are making together in a creative tension. Among other things, this is a mindfulness practice involving "going into" the complexity of the situation and staying in that complexity. This requires holding in tension the emotions, thoughts, perspectives, etc. coming from each of us throughout the conversation.

I also used the daisy model to imagine this person in his fuller complexity. I know that some of his early life experiences have been profound shapers in his current way of handling difficult situations. Using the daisy reminded me that my experience of him is a slice of a much more complex person.

I reminded myself of my commitment to practice mystery before every conversation that we would have about the issue. And because his default response is to physically walk away or mentally check out, I spent time imagining how I would act into the situation that honored my commitment to him, to me, and to the resolution of the issue. Doing this imaginary exercise helped me anticipate some of the bifurcation points that would no doubt occur.

In practice, this meant that I called him out when I noticed him checking out. This happened a few times, when, for instance, he would say something like, "I don't understand why this matters and I really don't want to take the time to understand it." I'd call him on it by saying something like, "you're checking out on me. You're a smart person and this issue isn't rocket science. I'm not going to let you off the hook here..." and then I'd go on to explain (again) why this matters. I talked about it in two ways—one aspect is the legal ramification of not acting and the second is the relational ramifications with his family if he doesn't act. Throughout the conversation, I was like a laser beam—

penetrating and unrelenting, but never rude. I didn't back down and I said several times, "you're leaving me again—don't do it" and a few times, "did you just hear what you said?" How do you think your kids would respond if they heard you say that?"

We made progress toward a resolution in each conversation we had. But the progress was slow and we always seemed to start back at square one with his opening remarks of, I really don't understand why this matters and I really don't want to take care of this. When this theme emerged over and over again, I began to think about the LUUUUTT model in terms of the unknown, unheard, and untellable stories. As I tried to put myself in his position, I think the big untellable story was about "saving face". He made a big mistake at one time and it was embarrassing to admit it to his family. I could really understand how difficult it can be to admit a mistake to the people that you love, knowing that your mistake affects them in significant ways. One of the things we talked about was not needing to frame the issue as "I screwed up" but instead to frame it as "making it right". This change of frame was crucial in seeing a dignified way forward for him.

What I'm about to say now is difficult to describe so bear with me. At the level of feelings, when I was acting out of the highest level context of mystery, the anger, resentment and lack of respect that I was experiencing was more porous than solid. It felt like it was moving *through* me rather than holding itself in a place in my body (my chest or my stomach or my head…). These emotions were energetic and moving because I was allowing them to be in a larger context of self, other, and compassion.

Our conversations led to his agreement to have a family meeting in which I would explain what should have been done financially eight years ago and what he is doing now to make the situation right. He was quite agitated leading up to the conversation. But in the family meeting, I framed the issue as he and I had talked about; that of making things right. His family responded very positively and he was a different person (light, playful, funny) by the time the conversation was over.

At that moment, the issue was gone…for him…and for me. My deep anger, resentment, and disgust were transformed into something much closer to compassion and love. I was surprised at how quickly compassion and love showed up. This was a moment of big M mystery! My part was committing to a practice of keeping little m mystery as a highest level of context and acting into that story as best I could. So, in this situation what did that mean?

I went into my anger and resentment. I didn't push it away. I looked at it, I owned it, I brought it into my conversations with him but in the context of mystery as the guiding story. I didn't let it "own me" but I used it as a penetrating guide for how to act in the next turn, and then the next one, and the one after that.... And throughout my many conversations with him over this matter, I have held my ground. I also listened deeply to him...and to what he isn't saying or can't say. I felt the untellable story of his embarrassment at not taking care of this many years ago and his fear that his family members wouldn't respect him. As he became more complex to me in the stories that I knew he *wasn't* telling, my own feelings for him became more nuanced and open.

We made a better social world! I also believe that my years of practicing the kinds of exercises that are in this book enabled me to create a scaffold for both of us to act into. We co-constructed the conversations and eventual good outcome together...and I had some tools, skills, and a commitment to make a better social world that helped us both navigate a very difficult situation. I am fairly certain that this would not have happened without my commitment to use the tools and models of CMM.

This example is the stuff of our lives. And the more tools we have to stay open, to stay mindful, and to honor the complexity of self, others, and the situation, the better off we'll be. Having said that, I also recognize that this level of intentionality does not come easily. I'm hearing the voice of my former Aikido teacher who said about the practices of Aikido, "become a black belt, practice 10,000 times and you will be ready to begin." The learning for me in that paradoxical statement is that it is not the destination that we are seeking, it is the doing...over and over and over again. And as we continue to practice, we will become better at seeing the nuance, beauty, and complexity of our social worlds and of acting skillfully and compassionately into them.

You and I have meandered as I have sat in my courtyard recounting dreams, fears, vulnerabilities, and the compassionate embrace of Mystery. And we have now arrived into town. But it is just one town. And you will soon leave it and continue the journey that will ultimately take you to another town...and then another. Remember to meander and embrace and celebrate the journey. There is a poem in the town square called, *Remembering*. Take this with you as you set out for home...

Love

is Divinity's way

of reminding us of

Mystery.

Remember

—kim pearce

Endnotes

[i] Pema Chodron (2009), *Taking the Leap: Freeing Ourselves from Old Habits and Fears*. Boston: Shambhala Publications. p. 87

[ii] Robyn's Penman's (2000) *Reconstructing Communicating: Looking to a future* (LEA Publisher) provides a clear and informative historical overview of the role of Locke, Hume and other enlightenment thinkers in defining and conceptualizing communication.

[iii] John Dewey (1891), Moral theory and practice, *International journal of ethics:* I: 186-203. (quotation on p 200).

[iv]see http://video.google.com/videoplay?doc id=8842256077873416888 to view the video, Powers of 10.

Kimberly Pearce was Professor of Communication at De Anza College for more than 25 years. She is a cofounder of two non-profit 501(c)(3) organizations and a consulting business—the Public Dialogue Consortium, the CMM Institute for Personal and Social Evolution, and Pearce Associates. All three organizations are in service of creating better patterns of communication in private and public settings. Additionally, the CMM Institute is the promoter and connector of all things related to the communication theory, the Coordinated Management of Meaning (CMM).

Kim's commitments as a practitioner and researcher involve the connections among Buberian dialogue, adult transformational learning, interpersonal neuroscience, and the Coordinated Management of Meaning theory as leverages for creating more inclusive, compassionate, and reflexive ways of being and acting in a globalized, post-modern world. She has authored a book on *Public Engagement and Civic Maturity*, a book of illustrated poetry, *Nine Lives*, and has coauthored along with Barnett Pearce and Jesse Sostrin, *CMM Solutions*. Additionally, she has written and coauthored a number of book chapters and articles. Her work as a practitioner includes a number of projects in the United States, as well as in Argentina, Brazil, Colombia, Denmark, Egypt, England, France, Greece, and Ireland.

Kim has three adult children who also happen to be very special friends, six grandchildren, and a floppy-eared four-legged companion. She lives just outside of Tucson, Arizona.